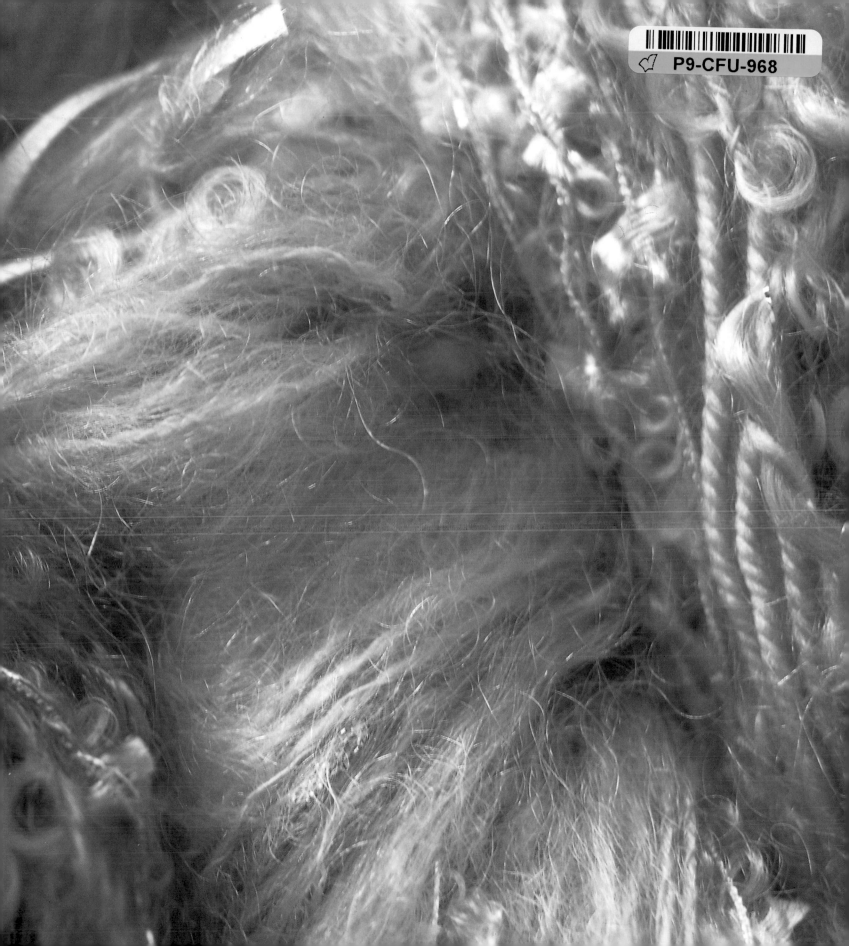

Pretty Knits

30 Designs from Loop in London

Susan Cropper

Photography by Vanessa Davies

POTTER
CRAFT
New York

Published in the United States by Potter Craft,
an imprint of the Crown Publishing Group, a
division of Random House, Inc., New York.
www.crownpublishing.com
www.pottercraft.com

Originally published in Great Britain as *Loop:
Pretty Knits* by Jacqui Small, LLP, London.

POTTER CRAFT and CLARKSON N. POTTER
are trademarks, and POTTER and colophon are
registered trademarks of Random House, Inc.

Library of Congress Cataloging-in-Publication
Data is available upon request

ISBN-13: 978-0-307-38315-0

Printed in China

10 9 8 7 6 5 4 3 2 1

First American Edition

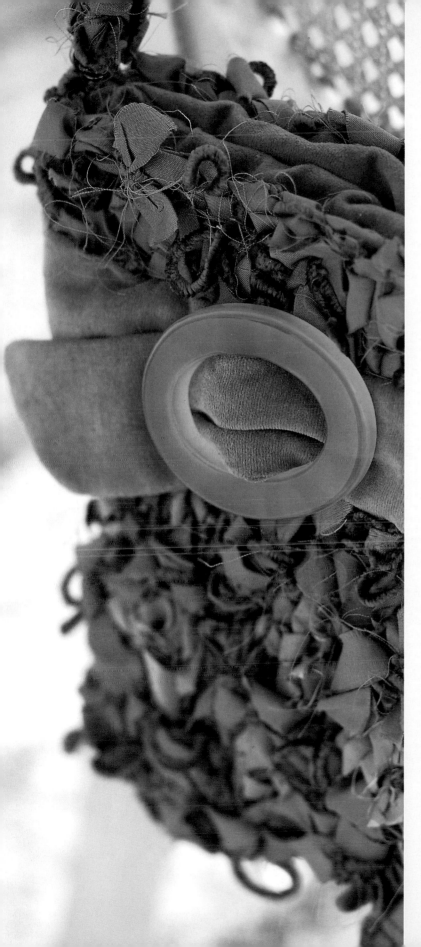

Contents

Introduction 6

Pretty, Gorgeous, Yummy Yarns 8

Flirty Fashionista 12
Super-glam garments for stylish chicks

Divine Accessories 54
Pretty fashion pieces for every occasion

Beautiful Boudoirs 82
Indulgent furnishings for sensuous bedrooms

Feminine Fripperies 104
Gorgeous accessories for anywhere in the home

Techniques 128

Suppliers 140

Designers' Biographies 142

Acknowledgments 144

Introduction

My customers at Loop in London often ask for patterns for the garments, housewares, and other objects that they see around the shop. Usually, we have to tell them that they're made by independent designers and we're sorry, but there is no pattern available. Finally, now there is.

When I first dreamed of opening Loop in London, in the summer of 2005, it was important to me that it be a place full of warmth and charm, beauty and inspiration—an inviting space where people could come to browse, buy, learn, talk, and feel inspired by all things to do with knitting. As a knitter and devoted yarn junkie, I had found it frustrating that there was no shop in London that reflected the new-found interest in this traditional craft and the exciting developments that have consequently been made. There was nowhere that offered anything but a small selection of the amazing array of yarns that are now available, or lessons that went beyond beginners, or knitted

clothes, housewares, accessories, and quirky objects created by the wealth of talented young designers who are working in knitting today. This is what I set out to achieve with Loop—a welcoming, friendly, and informal space, where everything to do with knitting was available under one roof—from tiny vintage buttons, useful and unusual notions, a stunning selection of exquisite yarns, patterns, books, and the finished work of brilliant designers and makers, to lessons and workshops for all levels.

After a lot of hard work, laughter, and joy, I am proud to say that we have realized a large part of that dream. The shelves are piled high with endless different yarns from the U.K., North and South America, Continental Europe, Australia, South Africa, and Japan. We have everything from the simplest basic natural yarn to the kookiest hand-dyed handspuns. This variety reflects my passion for fiber, color, and texture and my desire to kindle this love for yarn in other people.

The most amazing thing about knitting is that it basically consists of two sticks and a ball of yarn (or fabric, or ribbon, or anything else you may want to experiment with—but more of that later), and you can go anywhere you want with it, from the simplest garter-stitch scarf to the most elaborate garment or throw; it is all possible with the same basic tools. What has been an incredible privilege for me at Loop is to meet a host of talented young designers who have reclaimed this craft and made it their own. Their unique designs are an inspiration and a cause to celebrate. All of the designers who have contributed patterns to this book have a connection with Loop in London: some sell their finished work in the shop; others teach the workshops; or we might stock their wonderful patterns or their fabulous yarns.

Left and opposite: Views of the Loop shop in London with some of the gorgeous yarns and accessories on display.

I hope that *Pretty Knits* will provide you with a set of great patterns from a host of talented designers, offering you everything from corsages to cushions. Some of the patterns are fairly quick and simple for beginner knitters who just crave a little nudge to try out shaping or new stitches. Others are more challenging, like Louisa Harding's exquisite "Cameo" Shawl (see pages 64-67) or Ruth Cross's "Isobel" Gilet (see pages 30-35). These will both demand your utmost attention, but the results will be well worth it—they are among the things that have made us gasp in admiration as each new sample came in. There is an array of projects to choose from—clothes and accessories, such as tops, bags, brooches, wraps, and shawls, as well as cute cushions, divine throws, and other gorgeous items for the home.

Although it is sometimes wonderful to find a pattern one loves and then knit away, it becomes a whole different experience when you feel confident enough to use the pattern but work with another color, or even a different yarn altogether (of course, as long as it has the same gauge and a fairly similar fiber content). But that is when knitting can become a live thing, when it is fairly fluid and you can put some of yourself into the making. For example, if you're making a cardigan fastened with five buttons, you might say to yourself, "Actually, I think I'll find a vintage brooch or kilt pin and just hold it together that way." Or you might decide to embellish the edge of a blanket or throw with a different color or stitch, or a cluster of bobbles. I hope that you'll gain the confidence, and feel inspired, to make the patterns in this book your own, by experimenting with yarn, color, and embellishment.

Once you set your heart on making one of the patterns, I suggest you read through it before you begin, to get a feel for what is involved. If there is a technique used with which you are unfamiliar, see pages 128-40, where we have given step-by-step instructions for some of the trickier techniques. It's always a good idea to practice on a swatch first to get to grips with a new stitch. Keep your swatch to refer to later. This is also a nice way to start building up a personal swatch library.

So, this book is a little extension of Loop and those who make it special. We hope you find some inspiration here to make some pretty wonderful things for yourself and others. The original patterns that follow have all been designed by people I have enormous respect for. Working with them, both at Loop in London and in the creation of this book, continues to be a joy, and I hope that you will love the following designs as much as we do. Happy knitting!

Pretty, Gorgeous, Yummy Yarn

"Oohs" and "Aahhs" are often heard as knitters wander around my London shop, Loop, which brims with more than 130 different yarns. Gorgeous yarns are what inspired me to open Loop, and they are still the heart of the shop. Constantly trying to source ever-more-beautiful yarns for customers is my driving force. When I go to trade fairs in Europe or the United States, I am truly in yarn heaven, surrounded by endless aisles of merinos, mohairs, hand-dyes, handspuns, bouclés, tweeds, ribbons, chenilles, bamboos, cashmeres, alpacas, and silks—I could swoon. After carefully selecting yarns that will eventually fill a shelf back in London, I think about them for weeks or sometimes months until the new deliveries arrive. When the truck pulls up and we see what's inside, it's like a birthday celebration for us. I know other yarn junkies out there will understand.

There is truly a sense of joy in sourcing the most exquisite and unique yarns. It is always a lovely moment, too, when a customer has found something new when traveling—to the Shetland Islands, for example,

or farther afield—and they bring it into the shop to show us. Sometimes those yarns end up on the shelves, too—it's very much a fluid thing. Yarns originate from all over the British Isles, North and South America, Continental Europe, Australia, South Africa, and Japan. The choice is astounding, and they all have their own soul and character—from Debbie Bliss's subdued duck-egg palette, Blue Sky Alpacas's hand-dyes, and the whimsical vibrancy of Louisa Harding's yarns to Habu's "Fringe Tape Ribbon", sourced from a small mill in rural Japan.

I also think of the independent yarn spinners and dyers—Gina Wilde, of Alchemy Yarn in California, handpainting her silks in the sunshine; Jane Saffir, of Jade Sapphire; Nadine Curtis, of Be Sweet; and Takako Ueki, of Habu, overseeing hand-dyeing in South Africa, Mongolia, and Japan. There has also been a great resurgence of people spinning and dyeing yarn in small cottage industries. They are too numerous to name, but the sheer range and quality of their yarn is an indication of the energy and excitement surrounding yarn today. Lexi Boeger, of PluckyFluff, is a great example of how far the idea of what yarn can be has been pushed: Each skein of her unique yarn tells a story. She handspins her yarn and throws in the most gorgeous combinations of felted flowers, beads, sequins, pompoms, buttons, cloth, and bobbles. For all of these people, their devotion to their craft is obvious by the sheer beauty of the yarns they produce. In the morning when I open up the shop and get it ready for the day, I am still overwhelmed at times by the beauty of the little gems lining the shelves before me.

These days, knitting isn't done out of economic necessity. When cheap, stylish clothing is readily available from chain stores, there is no need to invest the time required to create something if you are

Left: Nothing beats the drape and luscious feel of silk yarn, available in an incredible range of colors. Here are examples of handpainted silk and silk blends—Alchemy Yarns "Synchronicity" in Silver (far left) and Citrine (far right), and "Silk Purse" in Silver (second right), with Debbie Bliss "Pure Silk" in Plum and Cream (second left).

Opposite: Shimmering ribbon yarns can be used as an embellishment or edging to add beauty to your knits, or be threaded through a row of eyelet stitches, such as in Debbie Bliss's "Bliss" Empire-Line Top (see pages 18-21). These ribbon yarns are exquisite—Colinette "Giotto" (top left), Leigh Radford for Lantern Moon "Silk Gelato" (top right), and Knit One, Crochet Too "Tartelette" (foreground).

Opposite: These yarns are full of nubbly texture and luscious color, from Gedifra "Sheela" (background) to Ozark Handspun, the most unusual and most saturated color of the hand-dyes and handspuns (center) and Colinette hand-dyed "Graffiti" (foreground).

Right: The cosiest, chunkiest yarns—Blue Sky Alpacas "Bulky" in Polar (top) and "Bulky Hand-Dyes" in Light Blue (bottom), and KnitGlobal "Chunky" in Pink Sherbert (center), an incredibly soft, superfine Australian merino wool, dyed in natural or organic plant-based dyes. These yarns are great for everything from bulky, quick-knit scarves to beautiful throws.

going to knit with a bad acrylic that won't last beyond its first wash (though some acrylics are truly lovely—ggh "Amelie" yarn feels like angora, honest!). Whatever yarn you choose, try to buy the best quality your budget allows. So much time goes into making the knitted piece that your work deserves the best materials. I am sure the increased popularity of knitting is partly due to knitters' being seduced by the yarns—the luscious or subtle colors and the myriad textures. Who wouldn't be? After all, knitting shops today are as beautiful and enticing as pastry shops. My greatest pleasure is when someone comes into the shop, tagging along with a friend who knits, and is so excited by the colors and choice of textures that she decides right there and then to learn to knit. Wonderful!

Yarn comes from sheep, rabbits, alpacas, silkworms, goats, cotton, hemp, flax, bark, recycled fabric, and acrylics; there is wool, merino wool, mohair, cashmere, angora, silk, linen, bamboo, paper, steel wrapped with silk, stainless-steel wire, and an endless variety of blends of these fibers available as yarn. Yarn from rare breeds, as well as handspun and hand-dyed, Fair-Trade, and organic yarns are also growing in variety as well as accessibility. In addition, you can experiment with knitting using fabric torn into strips and tied together. Vintage fabric or ribbon is great for this and makes a lovely edging for a throw or blanket.

There are many different weights of yarn to choose from. Traditional European yarns such as laceweight, 4-ply, and double knitting (or DK), are now taking their place in the United States, alongside their slightly heavier American counterparts, sport weight and worsted weight. There are Aran/fisherman yarns and chunky/bulky yarns. You can often substitute one yarn for another of similar weight and fiber, as long as you can achieve the gauge stated in the pattern. If you can't find the yarn specified for a pattern, have a good look around

and try a similar one that you love and that will work well in that design. First, though, knit up a swatch (see page 132), as you may need to adjust the needle size.

All the yarns chosen for the projects in this book are gorgeous and easy to work with. They complement the patterns and add that extra something to an already beautiful design. They are some of our favorite yarns, from the cozy chunkiness of alpaca and wool to the shimmering strips of Leigh Radford's exquisite "Silk Gelato" yarn, made from Vietnamese silk.

One last thing—if you are lucky enough to have a good yarn store in your area, support it! The owners will have a unique passion for choosing the yarns they stock that a department store or anonymous Internet site can never equal. An independent shop has the commitment needed to keep trying to find the next wonderful gadget or glorious yarn. And there is nothing like seeing the colors, touching the fibers, and holding them against you to check out both the "tickle factor" and how really soft they are. Conversations spring up among customers about tricky patterns and stitch techniques, and knitting help is always on hand. Plus, you'll also be able to find out when the next shipment of a gorgeous new yarn is coming in.

flirty fashionista

t his gorgeous camisole in a delicate shade of pinky lilac would be a welcome addition to any girl's wardrobe. The smocked top is decorated with small, sparkly glass seed beads in shades of pink, lilac, and cream, which add just the right touch of opulence above the narrowly ribbed body.

Beaded Camisole   Leslie Scanlon

MATERIALS

3 (4, 4, 5) 1¾oz (50g) balls ggh Merino Soft, shade 82
Pair each Size 6 (4mm) and 7 (4.5mm) knitting needles
One each Size 6 (4mm) and 7 (4.5mm) circular needle,
    24 inches (60cm) long
Two Size 6 (4mm) double-pointed needles
Size G/6 (4.5mm) crochet hook
Elastic thread
150–200 glass beads in shades of pink, lilac, and cream,
    approximately 2–3mm
Additional round and/or bugle beads to decorate the straps or to use
    end to end along the purl rows under the bodice (optional)
Small, thin sewing needle that will go through the hole of each bead
Transparent sewing thread or thread that matches yarn color

MEASUREMENTS

To fit bust

32	34	36	38 inches
81	86	91	97cm

Finished length to bodice

9¾	10¾	11½	12 inches
25	28	29	30cm

GAUGE

31 sts and 28 rows = 4 inches (10cm) square measured over K2, P1 rib
on Size 6 needles or the size required to obtain the correct gauge.
24 sts and 28 rows = 4 inches (10cm) square measured over K1, P3 rib
on Size 7 needles or the size required to obtain the correct gauge.

ABBREVIATIONS

See page 129.

BODY

Using the Size 6 circular needle, cast on 240(255, 270, 285) sts.
Join for knitting in the round and PM at the beginning of the round (center back).

Round 1 * K2, P1; rep from * to end.
Repeating this round forms K2, P1 rib.
Cont in rib until work measures 9(10, 10½, 11) inches/23(25.5, 27, 28)cm.

Change to Size 7 circular needle.
Next round (decrease round) * K3, K2tog tbl; rep from * to end.
192(204, 216, 228) sts.
Knit 2(2, 3, 3) rounds.
Purl 3(3, 4, 4) rounds.
Knit 2(2, 3, 3) rounds.
Next round (RS) * P3, K1; rep from * until 104(108, 116, 120) sts [half the total number of sts plus 8(6, 8, 6) sts for the crossover at the center front of the bodice] in all have been worked. 88(96, 100, 108) sts remain unworked. Turn (do not wrap stitch) and continue to work back and forth in rows.
Next row (WS) P2 (left front edge), continue in K1, P3 rib, knitting the knit sts and purling the purl sts as they occur, until all 104(108, 116, 120) sts have been worked, and then continue in the same rib pattern to the right side center front. Turn and cast on 8 sts. 200(212, 224, 236) sts. Continue working in rows over all stitches.
Next row (RS) K2 (right front edge), maintaining the continuity of the rib, rib to last 2 sts, K2.
Next row (WS) P1 (left front edge), sl1, work 1 st, psso, rib to last 2 sts, P2. 199(211, 223, 235) sts.
Next row (RS) K1, sl1, work 1 st, psso, rib to last 2 sts, K2. 198(210, 222, 234) sts.
Rep the last 2 rows 6(6, 8, 8) times. 186(198, 206, 218) sts.
Next row (WS) P1, sl1, work 1 st, psso, rib 41(43, 43, 45), P2, bind off 94(102, 110, 118) sts in rib, sl1, work 1 stitch, psso, rib 41(43, 43, 45), P2. Continue to work on right front bodice only. 45(47, 47, 49) sts.
** **Next row (RS)** K1, sl1, work 1 st, psso, rib to last 2 sts, K2.
44(46, 46, 48) sts.
Next row (WS) P1, sl1, work 1 st, psso, rib to last 2 sts, P2.
43(45, 45, 47) sts.
Rep last 2 rows until 3(3, 5, 5) sts rem.
Cut yarn and thread tail through rem sts, draw up and secure. **

With RS facing, rejoin yarn to left front bodice. 45(47, 47, 49) sts.
Work as for right front bodice from ** to **.

STRAPS (Make 2)

Using a Size 6 double-pointed needles, cast on 4 sts.
Work an I-cord (see page 136) for the desired length.
The straps can tie at the back neck, crisscross at the center back, or simply go from front to back.

FINISHING

Bottom Ruffle

With RS facing, using a Size 6 circular needle, pick up the original 240(255, 270, 285) cast-on sts. Join for knitting in the round and PM at the beginning of the round.
Round 1 Knit.
Round 2 Inc 1 in every st. 480(510, 540, 570) sts.
Round 3 Knit.
Bind off.
Weave in all ends.
Gently block to shape following the instructions on page 138 and referring to the yarn label.

Crochet Edging

With RS facing, using a Size G/6 crochet hook and starting at the center right front, work a row of single crochet up and down the right front bodice, across the back and then up and down the left front bodice.

Beading

Work one front at a time. Starting with the first two knit columns at the center front edge of the left front bodice, count up two stitches in each knit column. With needle and thread, sew the two knit stitches together, circling the stitches twice. It is not necessary to pull the stitch tight. Without cutting the thread, sew on a bead, then secure the thread at the back. Next, count up four rows in the second and third knit columns and sew together, incorporating a bead. Continue working either across the columns or up and down, alternating every four stitches until the entire bodice is covered (see photograph, opposite).
Sew the eight stitches cast on for the center front right bodice into position, underlapping the left front bodice.
The band of purl stitches under the bodice may be beaded with contrasting bugle beads or more of the same beads used in the bodice. Beads can also be added to the straps.
Weave elastic thread through the backs of both bands of knit stitches under the bodice.
Attach straps.

the great empire-line shape of this cute cap-sleeve top in a vibrant shade of blue is emphasized by the contrasting leaf-green ribbon threaded through the eyelet ridge. The "skirt" is worked in stockinette stitch, while the yoked top features pretty bird's-eye spots. Sweet detailing and gorgeous fresh colors combine to make this a must-have top.

"Bliss" Empire-Line Top Debbie Bliss

MATERIALS
8(9, 10) 1¾oz (50g) balls Debbie Bliss Cathay, shade 07 Teal (Yarn A)
Small ball of smooth contrasting yarn (Yarn B) (see note below)
Pair each Size 3 (3.25mm) and 5 (3.75mm) knitting needles
One Size 3 (3.25mm) circular needle, 24 inches (60cm) long
Stitch holders
Row counter
1⅝ yards (1.5m) green double-sided silk ribbon, ¼ inch (5mm) wide

MEASUREMENTS
To fit bust

32-34	36-38	40-42 inches
81-86	92-97	102-107cm

Actual size

36	40	44 inches
92	102	112cm

Sleeve seam length

1½	1½	1½ inches
4	4	4cm

GAUGE
22 sts and 30 rows = 4 inches (10cm) square over stockinette stitch using Size 5 needles or the size required to obtain the correct gauge.

ABBREVIATIONS
See page 129.

NOTES
The contrasting yarn is used only to work a temporary edging, which is removed on completion to reveal a scalloped edge.

BACK
Using Size 3 needles and Yarn B, cast on 125(137, 149) sts.
** Row 1 P1, * K1 tbl, P1; rep from * to end.
Row 2 K1, * P1 tbl, K1; rep from * to end.
Repeating rows 1 and 2 form twisted rib.
Cut Yarn B.

Change to Yarn A.
Work 2 more rows in twisted rib.

Change to Size 5 needles.
Work 12 rows stockinette stitch, beg with a knit row.
Next row (decrease row) (RS) K4, skpo, knit to last 6 sts, K2tog, K4. 123(135, 147) sts.
Work 11 rows st-st, beg with a purl row.
Rep the last 12 rows 4 times then the decrease row once more. ** 113(125, 137) sts.
Cont straight in st-st until back measures 11(11½, 12) inches/ 28(29, 30)cm from beg of Yarn A, ending with a purl (WS) row.

Change to Size 3 needles.
Yoke decrease row (RS) K42(45, 51), [K2tog, K1] 10(12, 12) times, K41(44, 50). 103(113, 125) sts.
Next row Knit.
*** Eyelet row (RS) K2(3, 3), * bring yarn from back to front over needle, P2tog, take yarn to back between sts; rep from * to last 1(2, 2) sts, K1(2, 2).
Next row P2(3, 3), * P1 tbl, P1; rep from * to last 1(2, 2) sts, P1(2, 2).
Next row (RS) Purl.

Change to Size 5 needles.

Work 3 rows in st-st, beg with a purl row.

Next row (RS) K3(4, 2), * P1, K3; rep from * to last 4(5, 3) sts, P1, K3(4, 2).

Work 3 rows in st-st.

Next row (RS) K1(2, 4), *P1, K3; rep from * to last 2(3, 5) sts, P1, K1(2, 4).

The last 8 rows form bird's-eye spot pattern.

Cont in patt until back measures 13¾(14½, 15¼) inches/35(37, 39)cm from beg of Yarn A, ending with a WS row.

Shape raglan armholes

Maintain continuity of bird's-eye spot pattern.

Bind off 5(6, 7) sts at beg of next 2 rows. 93(101, 111) sts.

Next row K2, skpo, patt to last 4 sts, K2tog, K2. 91(99, 109) sts.

Next row P2, P2tog, purl to last 4 sts, P2tog tbl, P2. 89(97, 107) sts.

Rep the last 2 rows 7(6, 5) times. 61(73, 87) sts.

Next row K2, skpo, patt to last 4 sts, K2tog, K2.

Next row Purl.

Rep the last 2 rows to 45(49, 53) sts.

Leave sts on a holder.

FRONT

Using Size 3 needles and Yarn B, cast on 147(161, 177) sts.

Work as for back from ** to **. 135(149, 165) sts.

Cont in st-st until front measures 11(11½, 12) inches/28(29, 30)cm from beg of Yarn A, ending with a purl (WS) row.

Change to Size 5 needles.

Yoke decrease row (RS) K20(21, 23) sts, [K2tog, K1] 32(36, 40) times, K19(20, 22). 103(113, 125) sts.

Next row Knit.

Work as for back from *** to end.

SLEEVES

Using Size 3 needles and Yarn A, cast on 73(79, 85) sts.

Row 1 (WS) Knit.

Row 2 (Eyelet row) (RS) K3, * bring yarn from back to front over needle, P2tog, take yarn to back between sts; rep from * to last 2 sts, K2.

Row 3 P3, * P1tbl, P1; rep from * to last 2 sts, P2.

Row 4 (RS) Purl.

Change to Size 5 needles.

Work 3 rows in st-st, beg with a purl row.

Next row K4(2, 4), * P1, K3, rep from * to last st, K1.

Work 3 rows in st-st.

Next row K2(4, 2), * P1, K3, rep from * to last 3 sts, P1, K2.

The last 8 rows form bird's-eye spot pattern.

Next row Purl.

Shape armholes and sleeve top

Maintain continuity of bird's-eye spot pattern.

Bind off 5(6, 7) sts at beg of next 2 rows.

Next row K2, skpo, patt to last 4 sts, K2tog, K2.

Work 3 rows in patt.

Rep the last 4 rows 7(9, 11) times. 47 sts.

Leave sts on a holder.

NECK EDGE

Block each piece following the instructions on page 138 and referring to the yarn label.

Join raglan seams.

With RS facing, using the Size 3 circular needle and beg at left back raglan, ** [P2tog, P43, P2tog] across 47 sts of left sleeve, then [P2tog, P41(45, 49), P2tog] across 45(49, 53) sts of front; rep from ** across right sleeve and back. 176(184, 192) sts.

PM to indicate beg of round.

Round 1 Take yarn to back of work, * bring yarn from back to front over needle, P2tog, take yarn to back between sts; rep from * to marker.

Round 2 Knit across all stitches, working into back of the yo of the previous row.

Bind off purlwise.

FINISHING

Remove Yarn B carefully to reveal a picot edge.

Join sleeve and side seams.

Thread ribbon through eyelet row at start of yoke on front and back, with ribbon ends at center front.

We are delighted that Amy Twigger Holroyd applied her unique technique of joined-up seams to a handknitted piece so we can make her designs, too. This swing cardigan reflects her signature effortless style, and the bulky yarn makes it knit up fairly quickly. Keep it simple, or knit a corsage to embellish it.

"Elsie" Swing Cardigan   Amy Twigger Holroyd

MATERIALS

8(9) 3½oz (100g) balls Rowan Big Wool, shade 20 Lucky

Pair Size 15 (10mm) knitting needles

Pair Size 19 (12mm) knitting needles

Stitch holders or set of four Size 19 (12mm) double-pointed needles (to hold stitches)

Row counter

MEASUREMENTS

To fit bust

32-36	36-40 inches
81-91	91-102cm

Length to center back

20½	22 inches
52	56cm

Sleeve seam length

12	13 inches
30	33cm

GAUGE

14 sts and 17 rows = 6 inches (15cm) square measured over stockinette stitch on Size 19 needles or the size required to obtain the correct gauge.

ABBREVIATIONS

See page 129.

K4tog Knit 4 stitches together

FRONT PANELS (Make 2)

Using Size 19 needles, cast on 42(50) sts.

Row 1 * K2, P2; rep from * to last 2 sts, K2.

Row 2 P1, * K2, P2; rep from * to last st, K1.

Row 3 * P2, K2; rep from * to last 2 sts, P2.

Row 4 K1, * P2, K2; rep from * to last st, P1.

These 4 rows form diagonal rib.

Row 5-14(16) Repeat rows 1-4 two(3) times and rows 1-2 one(-) times.

Next row (RS) K1, skpo -(1) time, knit to last 3 sts, K2tog -(1) time, K1. 42(48) sts.

Work 25 rows in st-st, beg with a purl row.

Do not bind off. Leave stitches on a holder or Size 19 double-pointed needle.

BACK PANEL

Using Size 19 needles, cast on 86(98) sts.

Work 14(16) rows diagonal rib as given for the fronts.

Next row (RS) K1, skpo, knit to last 3 sts, K2tog, K1. 84(96) sts.

Work 25 rows in st-st, beg with a purl row.

Do not bind off. Leave stitches on a holder or Size 19 double-pointed needle.

SLEEVES (Make 2)

Using Size 19 needles, cast on 38(42) sts.

Work 14(16) rows diagonal rib as given for fronts.

Row 15(17) Knit.

Row 16(18) Purl.

Repeat these 2 rows -(1) time.

Row 17(21) K1, skpo, knit to last 3 sts, K2tog, K1. 36(40) sts.

Rows 18-24(22-28) Work 7 rows in st-st, beg with a purl row.

Rows 25-32(29-36) Repeat rows 17-24(21-28) once. 34(38) sts.

Row 33(37) K1, skpo, knit to last 3 sts, K2tog, K1. 32(36) sts.

Row 34(38) Purl.

Do not bind off. Leave stitches on a holder or Size 19 double-pointed needle.

Join right front panel, right sleeve, and back

Row 35(39) (RS) With RS facing, hold right sleeve in your left hand and hold right front panel in your right hand. Slip 3 sts from front panel to LHN, K4tog (one stitch from sleeve and the 3 sts from front panel), knit to last st of sleeve and leave this st unworked on RHN. With RS facing, hold back panel in your left hand. Slip the last (unworked) stitch of sleeve onto LHN with the back panel sts and K4tog tbl (one stitch from sleeve and 3 sts from back panel). Do not knit to the end of the row. The joined right front panel and right sleeve sts are on RHN and the rem back panel sts are on LHN. Turn. 39(45) sts front panel, 32(36) sts sleeve, 81(93) sts back panel.

Row 36(40) Purl.

Rows 37-51(41-59) Repeat rows 35(39) and 36(40) 7(9) times and row 35(39) once more. 15(15) front panel sts, 32(36) sleeve sts, 57(63) back panel sts.

Row 52(60) P16(18) and work on these sleeve sts. Leave rem 16(18) sleeve sts and 15(15) front panel sts on a holder or Size 19 double-pointed needle.

Row 53(61) K15(17) sleeve sts. With RS facing, hold back panel in your left hand, slip last sleeve stitch onto LHN with the back panel sts and K4tog tbl. 16(18) sleeve sts, 54(60) back panel sts.

Row 54(62) Purl.

Row 55-61(63-69) Repeat last row 53(61) and 54(62) 3 times and row 53(61) once. 16(18) sleeve sts, 42(48) back panel sts.

Do not bind off. Cut yarn and leave stitches on a holder or Size 19 double-pointed needle.

With WS facing, rejoin yarn to the 16(18) unworked sleeve sts and 15(15) front panel sts left on a holder on row 52(60).

Row 1 (WS) Bind off 3 sts [slip first st], purl to end of sleeve. 13(15) sleeve sts.

Row 2 With RS facing, hold front panel in your right hand. Slip 3 sts from front panel to LHN, K4tog (one stitch from sleeve and the 3 sts from front panel), knit to end of sleeve. 13(15) sleeve sts, 12(12) front panel sts.

Row 3 Bind off 2(3) sts [slip first st], purl to end of sleeve. 11(12) sleeve sts.

Row 4 Repeat row 2. 11(12) sleeve sts, 9(9) front panel sts.

Row 5 Bind off 3 sts [slip first st], purl to end of sleeve. 8(9) sleeve sts.

Rows 6, 8, and 10 Repeat row 2.

Row 7 Repeat row 3. 6(6) sleeve sts, 6(6) front panel sts.

Row 9 Repeat row 5. 3(3) sleeve sts, 3(3) front panel sts.

Row 11 Bind off rem 3 sts [slip first st].

Join left front panel, left sleeve and back

Row 35(39) (RS) With RS facing, hold left sleeve in your left hand and hold back panel in your right hand. Slip 3 sts from back panel to LHN and K4tog (one stitch from sleeve and the 3 sts from back panel), knit to last st of sleeve and leave this unworked st on RHN. With RS facing, hold left front panel in your left hand. Slip the last (unworked) st of sleeve onto LHN with the left front panel sts and K4tog tbl (the one stitch from sleeve and 3 sts from front panel). Do not knit to the end of the row. The joined back panel and left sleeve sts are on RHN and the rem left front panel sts are on LHN. Turn. 39(45) front panel sts, 32(36) sleeve sts, 39(45) back panel sts.

Row 36(40) Purl to end of sleeve.

Rows 37-52(41-60) Repeat rows 35(39) and 36(40) rows 8(10) times. 15(15) front panel sts, 32(36) sleeve sts, 15(15) back panel sts.

Row 53(61) row With RS facing, hold back panel in your right hand, slip 3 sts from back panel to LHN, K4tog, K15(17). 16(18) sleeve sts, 12(12) back panel sts. Leave rem 16(18) sleeve sts and 15(15) rem front panel sts on a holder or Size 19 double-pointed needle.

Row 54(62) Purl to end of sleeve.

Row 55(63) With RS facing, hold back panel in your right hand. Slip 3 sts from back panel to LHN, K4tog, knit to end of row. 16(18) sleeve sts, 9(9) back panel sts.

Rows 56-61(64-69) Repeat rows 54(62) and 55(63) 3 times. 16(18) sleeve sts. 0(0) Back panel sts.

Do not bind off. Cut yarn and leave sts on a holder or Size 19 double-pointed needle.

With RS facing, rejoin yarn to the 16(18) unworked sleeve sts and 15(15) front panel sts left on stitch holder on row 53(61).

Row 1 (RS) Bind off 3 sts [slip first st], knit to last st of sleeve, slip 3 sts from front panel to LHN, slip last sleeve st from RHN to LHN and K4tog tbl. 13(15) sleeve sts, 12(12) front panel sts.

Rows 2, 4, 6, and 8 Purl to end of sleeve.

Row 3 Bind off 2(3) sts [slip first st], knit to last st of sleeve, slip 3 sts from front panel to LHN, slip last sleeve st from RHN to LHN and K4tog tbl. 11(12) sleeve sts, 9(9) front panel sts.

Row 5 Repeat row 1. 8(9) sleeve sts, 6(6) front panel sts.

Row 7 Repeat row 3. 6(6) sleeve sts, 3(3) front panel sts.

Row 9 Repeat row 5. 3(3) sleeve sts, 0(0) front panel sts.

Row 10 Bind off rem 3 sts purlwise [slip first st].

TIE

Using Size 15 needles, cast on 6 sts

Row 1 Sl1, K1, P2, K2.

Row 2 Sl1, K2, P2, K1.

Row 3 Sl1, P1, K2, P1, K1.

Row 4 Sl1, P2, K3.

Repeat rows 1-4 until the tie measures 59(61) inches/150(155)cm. Bind off.

FINISHING

Block each piece following the instructions on page 138 and referring to the yarn label.

Kitchener-stitch/graft center back (see pages 139-40).

Join side and sleeve seams.

With center of tie at center back neck, using backstitch sew the tie, slightly stretched, to the neck opening, beginning at the start of the yoke on each front.

based on a vintage French pattern, this adorable shrug is made in one piece, starting at the hem with a lacy floral motif and working up to the seed-stitch upper yoke.

"Avril" Shrug   Kristeen Griffin-Grimes for French Girl

MATERIALS

3(4, 4) 1¾oz (50g) balls Blue Sky Alpacas Alpaca Silk, shade 33 Ice

One each Size 4 (3.5mm) and 6 (4mm) circular needle
  (sharp-pointed for lacework), 24 inches (60cm) long

Set of four Size 6 (4mm) double-pointed needles (optional)

One Size F/5 (3.75mm) crochet hook

Two vintage buttons, ⅝ inches (15mm) diameter

Two buttons for reinforcing vintage buttons, ⅜ inch (10mm) diameter

2¼ yards (2m) pale blue silk or satin ribbon, ¼ inch (6mm) wide

Stitch holders and row counter

Stitch markers (split ring and regular)

MEASUREMENTS

To fit bust

32-34	36-38	40-42 inches
81-86	91-97	102-107cm

Actual size

35	40	44½ inches
89	102	114cm

Length to center back

12¼	13¼	14½ inches
31	34	37cm

Sleeve seam length

1¼	1¼	1¼ inches
3	3	3cm

GAUGE

17 sts and 28 rows = 4½ x 4 inches (11.5 x 10cm) over lace-stitch pattern (unblocked) using Size 6 needles or the size required to obtain the correct gauge.

ABBREVIATIONS

See page 129.

NOTES

Slip the markers when working across the rows.

When short-row shaping, refer to the wrapping technique on page 133.

The number of stitches changes over the rows.

LACE PATTERN SAMPLE SWATCH

Cast on 17 sts [12 sts for the lace pattern and 5 extra sts].

Row 1 (RS) K2, * K1, yo, skpo, K1, K2tog, yo; rep from * to last 3 sts, K3. 17 sts.

Row 2 and every alternate row Purl.

Row 3 K4, * yo, K3; rep from * to last st, K1. 21 sts.

Row 5 K2, K2tog, * yo, skpo, K1, K2tog, yo, s2kpo; rep from * to last 9 sts, yo, skpo, K1, K2tog, yo, skpo. K2. 17 sts.

Row 7 K2, * K1, K2tog, yo, K1, yo, skpo; rep from * to last 3 sts, K3. 17 sts.

Row 9 Repeat row 3. 21 sts.

Row 11 K2, * K1, K2tog, yo, s2kpo, yo, skpo; rep from * to last 3 sts, K3. 17 sts.

Row 12 Repeat row 2. 17 sts.

Rows 1-12 form the pattern.

BODICE

Using Size 6 circular needle and the cable method (see pages 130-31), cast on 5 sts, PM, cast on 125(143, 161) sts, PM, cast on 5 sts 135(153, 171) sts.

Row 1 (RS) * K1, P1; rep from * to last st, K1.

Row 2 Sl1P, * P1, K1; rep from * to last st, K1.

Repeating the row 2 forms seed stitch.

Rows 3-6 Repeat row 2.

Begin lace pattern

Row 1 Sl1P, [P1, K1] twice, SM, K2, * K1, yo, skpo, K1, K2tog, yo; rep from * to last 3 sts before marker, K3, SM, [K1, P1] twice, K1. 135(153, 171) sts.

Rows 2, 4, 6, 8, 10, and 12 Sl1P, [P1, K1] twice, purl to last 5 sts, [K1, P1] twice, K1.

Row 3 Sl1P, [P1, K1] twice, SM, K4, * yo, K3; rep from * to one st before marker, K1, SM, [K1, P1] twice, K1. 175(199, 223) sts.

Row 5 Sl1P, [P1, K1] twice, SM, K2, K2tog, * yo, skpo, K1, K2tog, yo,

s2kpo; rep from * to last 9 sts before marker, yo, skpo, K1, K2tog, yo, skpo, K2, SM, [K1, P1] twice, K1. 135(153, 171) sts.

Row 7 Sl1P, [P1, K1] twice, SM, K2, * K1, K2tog, yo, K1, yo, skpo; rep from * to 3 sts before marker, K3, SM, [K1, P1] twice, K1. 135(153, 171) sts.

Row 9 Repeat row 3. 175(199, 223) sts.

Row 11 Sl1P, [P1, K1] twice, SM, K2, * K1, K2tog, yo, s2kpo, yo, skpo; rep from * to last 3 sts before marker, K3, SM, [K1, P1] twice, K1. 135(153, 171) sts.

Rows 1-12 form the lace pattern.

Rows 12-54(60, 66) Repeat rows 1-12 of lace pattern 3(4, 4) times and rows 1-6 one(-, 1) time.

Adjust length here, ending 1 inch (2.5cm) below the armpit.

Each pattern repeat will add approx. 2 inches (5cm) to the length.

Change to seed stitch and mark position of sleeves

Row 1 (RS) Sl1P, * P1, K1; rep from * to last st, K1.
Repeating row 1 forms seed stitch.

Row 2 (WS) Repeat row 1, placing markers for the joining of the sleeves as follows: seed stitch 30(34, 38) sts, PM, seed st 8(8, 10) sts, PM, seed stitch 59(69, 75) sts, PM, seed stitch 8(8, 10) sts, PM, seed stitch rem 30(34, 38) sts. 135(153, 171) sts.
Do not cut yarn. Leave bodice stitches on a holder.

SLEEVES (Make 2)

The sleeves are worked in rounds.
Using a Size 6 circular needle or a set of four Size 6 double-pointed needles and the cable method (see pages 130-31), cast on 48(54, 60) sts. Join for knitting in the round and PM at beginning of round.

Round 1 * K1, K2tog, yo, K1, yo, skpo; rep from * end.

Round 2 K2, * yo, K3; rep from * to last st, yo, K1. 64(72, 80) sts.

Round 3 * K1, K2tog, yo, s2kpo, yo, skpo; rep from * to end. 48(54, 60) sts.

Round 4 * K1, P1; rep from * to end.

Round 5 (increase round) * [P1, K1] 8(9, 11) times, P0(1, 0), inc 1 in next 16(16, 16) sts, K0(1, 0), * [P1, K1], rep from * to end. 64(70, 76) sts.

Round 6 * K1, P1; rep from * to end.

Round 7 * P1, K1; rep from * to end.

Rounds 8-11 Repeat rounds 6 and 7 rounds twice.

Slip first 4(4, 5) sts of round onto a small holder and slip last 4(4, 5) sts of round onto a second small holder. Leave rem 56(62, 66) sts on a holder. Remove marker from sleeve.

Join sleeves to bodice

With RS facing, slip 30(34, 38) sts of right front bodice onto a Size 4 circular needle, SM, slip the next 8(8, 10) sts of the bodice onto a small holder, slip 56(62, 66) sts of the right sleeve onto the circular needle, SM, slip 59(69, 75) sts of the back bodice onto the circular needle, SM, slip the next 8(8, 10) sts of the bodice onto a small holder, slip 56(62, 66) sts of the left sleeve onto the circular needle, SM, slip 30(34, 38) sts of left front bodice onto the circular needle. 231(261, 283) sts on circular needle.

There should be 4 bodice markers where each of the sleeve edges meets the bodice.

Row 1 (RS) Using the ball of yarn left at right front bodice after marking the position of the sleeves, work across bodice in seed stitch, beginning with Sl1P, P1, K1, until one stitch before first marker, K2tog, continue to work across sleeve in seed stitch, until one stitch before second marker, K2tog, then continue across row and complete the last two joins in the same manner. 227(257, 279) sts.

On the following rows, the K2tog stitch just made will always be worked as a knit stitch on RS rows and as a purl stitch on WS rows. Raglan decreases will be made on both sides of this stitch on every RS row unless directed otherwise. Mark these K2tog stitches with split ring markers on RS and WS as you complete the first joining row.

Row 2 (WS) Sl1P, work in seed st while at the same time work the raglan line sts as P1.

Row 3 (RS) Sl1P, * work in seed stitch to 2 sts before the marked raglan line, keeping to pattern work K2tog or P2tog, K1 (raglan line), then keeping pattern correct K2tog or P2tog; rep from * to last raglan decrease has been completed, then work in seed stitch to end of row. 219(249, 271) sts.

Rows 4-22(26, 30) Repeat rows 2 and 3 nine(11, 13) times and row 2 once while at the same time make first buttonhole after working ¾(1¼, 1½) inches/2(3, 4)cm of seed-stitch yoke and the second at 1 inch/2.5cm after first buttonhole. 147(161, 167) sts.

Buttonhole row 1 (RS) Sl1P, P1, K1, P1, K2tog, yo, K1, patt to end.

Buttonhole row 2 (WS) Patt to yo of previous row, P1 into the yo, patt to end.

Shape front neck

Row 1 (RS) Do not cut yarn. Slip 14(16, 18) sts onto a holder for right front neck, join a new ball of yarn and skpo, patt to last 16(18, 20) sts, K2tog, turn and work on this set of 109(119, 121) sts. Leave rem 14(16, 18) sts on a second holder for left front neck.

Row 2 (WS) Sl1P, patt to end.

Shape sleeve tops

Maintain the continuity of the seed-stitch pattern, the raglan decreases, and the raglan lines.

Row 1 (RS) Skpo, ** patt to 4th stitch after the first raglan line, PM, patt to 5 sts before the next raglan line, turn, wrapping the stitch for short-row shaping (see page 133). PM between the stitch just wrapped and the last 4 sts before the second raglan line. Work short rows between the two markers as follows:

WS Patt to 1 st before marker, turn.

RS Patt to 2 sts before marker, turn.

WS Patt to 2 sts before marker, turn.

Cont working in short rows until the 10th(12th, 14th) short row has been completed and turning one stitch before the previous turn, thus ending with a WS row. There should be 5(5, 5) sts before the next marker before the last turn and RS facing after the last turn. Short-row shaping should measure approximately 1½(2, 2¼) inches/4(5, 5.5)cm. Adjust length here if necessary to bring the curve of the sleeve top to just over the shoulder, ending with RS facing after the last turn. Another 2 inches/5cm will be worked for the completion of the yoke. **

With RS facing, patt to 4 sts after the next raglan line and for the second sleeve repeat the instructions for first sleeve between ** and **, ending with a WS row and RS facing after the turn.

With RS facing, patt to last 2 sts, K2tog to complete row 1. 99(109, 111) sts.

Row 2 (WS) Patt across all 99(109, 111) stitches.

Row 3 Skpo, patt to last 2 sts, K2tog. 97(107, 109) sts.

Row 4 Patt.

Complete yoke

Try on garment to determine desired yoke length. Approximately ⅝ inch (1.5cm) will be added to the yoke length by the eyelet edging. If necessary, work extra rows, working skpo at right front edge and K2tog at left front edge on RS rows.

Yoke edging

With RS of garment facing, return to right front neck and pick up the yarn held with the set of 14(15, 16) sts at the start of the neck shaping.

Row 1 Sl1P, patt 11(12, 13) sts, K2tog (to maintain established patt), pick up 4 sts from row ends of right front yoke (if extra rows were worked pick up more sts in multiples of 2), patt to end of row, pick up 3 sts from row ends of left front yoke (if extra rows were worked pick up more sts in multiples of 2), slip 14(15, 16) sts from second holder to LHN, then pick up and work one more st from yoke edge together with the first st on LHN, patt across last 13(14, 15) sts. 133(145, 149) sts. Count all stitches and if necessary on next row equalize st count to a multiple of 2 + 1 for eyelet row by K2tog at center back.

Row 2 (WS) Sl1P, knit to end, adjusting the number of stitches as necessary.

Row 3 (eyelet row) (RS) * K2tog, yo; rep from * to last st, K1.

Row 4 Knit.

Bind off as follows:
* K2tog loosely, slip the stitch just made on the RHN back to the LHN; repeat from *. Do not cut yarn and use for front edging.

FRONT EDGINGS (Make 2)

With RS facing, using a F/5 crochet hook, work a row of single crochet in every slipped st along the front edge.

BUTTONS AND BUTTONHOLES

Using a crochet hook or threaded tapestry needle, work a round of single crochet or buttonhole stitch around buttonholes to reinforce opening.

FINISHING

Kitchener-stitch/graft (see pages 139-40) 8(8, 10) underarm sleeve stitches with 8(8, 10) underarm body stitches.

Lightly block the lower lace section (see page 138).

Overlap the first 3 eyelet holes of the right front neck over the first 3 eyelet holes of the left front neck. Using the buttonholes as guides, mark left front for button placement. Sew on buttons at marks, securing them with a smaller button on the underside.

Thread ribbon from right to left, starting with third eyelet on right side, passing it though the first left-side eyelet, which is directly underneath. Continue threading ribbon to end, passing it up through the third left eyelet and then first right eyelet. Tie into a bow to secure.

O h, the details! This exquisite cap-sleeve gilet is chock-full of them, knitted in a stunning mixture of bird cable and diamond patterning and fastened with a pretty velvet bow. The soft, pure wool yarn gives a great drape, and the pearly gray color makes it a very wearable design.

"Isobel" Gilet Ruth Cross

MATERIALS
8(9, 9) 1¾oz (50g) balls Rowan Pure Wool DK, shade 001 Clay
Pair Size 6 (4mm) knitting needles
Cable needle
Stitch/row markers
1 yard (1m) contrasting double-sided velvet ribbon, ⅝ inch (15mm) wide
Row counter

MEASUREMENTS
To fit bust
36	38	40 inches
91	97	102cm

Actual size
38	40	42½ inches
96	102	108cm

Length to shoulder
25¼	25½	25½ Inches
65	65	65cm

Sleeve seam
11.5	11.5	11.5cm
4½	4½	4½ inches

GAUGE
23 sts and 30 rows = 4 inches (10cm) square measured over stripe pattern on Size 6 needles or the size required to obtain the correct gauge.

ABBREVIATIONS
See page 129.
Cable 6 Slip next 2 stitches onto a cable needle and hold at back of work, K1 from LHN, K2 from cable needle, then slip next stitch onto a cable needle and hold at front of work, K2 from LHN, K1 from cable needle.
Sl6wyif Slip 6 stitches with yarn at front of work.
Sl6wyib Slip 6 stitches with yarn at back of work.

NOTES
It is essential to read the pattern before starting this project. It is also essential to keep track of rows and repeats. A row counter, stitch/row markers, and a notepad and pencil are recommended.

Ruth Cross uses the following techniques for casting on and knitting. It is recommended that these techniques be used for the Gilet and also for the Lavender Sleep Pillow (see pages 84–87). The results differ from those obtained by the common knitting methods.

CAST ON
Work the cast-on fairly tightly to give a firm edge.
1 Using the needles for the main knitting, tie the yarn around both needles.
2 Cross the needles with the right behind the left.
3 Make a loop and pull through (as though knitting through the back loop) and place this loop without twisting on the LHN. The RHN finishes behind the LHN, in the right place to make the next stitch.
4 Repeat step 3.

KNIT STITCHES
Knit stitches are worked through back of loop.
1 Insert RHN through back of loop.
2 Take yarn outside RHN then back between the needles and pull the loop through.
3 Repeat steps 1 and 2.

PURL STITCHES
Purl stitches are worked through the front of the loop.
1 Insert RHN through front of loop.
2 Take yarn from the front from right to left in front of both needles and then from left to right back between needles and pull the loop through.
3 Repeat steps 1 and 2.

When working stockinette stitch, the result will be similar to stockinette stitch worked in the normal way, but knitting 2 stitches together will mimic skpo.

YO (YARN OVER)
Between 2 knit stitches take yarn from back to front over RHN and back between the two.
Between 2 purl stitches take yarn from front to back over RHN and back between the two.
From a knit stitch to a purl stitch take yarn from back to front between needles, back to the back over the RHN and back between the two.
From a purl to a knit stitch take yarn from front to back between the needles, back over the RHN and back to the back between the two.

The number of stitches changes across the rows. The RS (knit) rows have extra stitches formed by the yo on the diamond repeats, but these are absorbed on the WS (purl) rows by the P2tog on the diamond repeats.

The garment is worked in one piece to the armholes.

The underlined stitches are the side stitches, and are so marked for ease of following the pattern. Experienced knitters may wish to extend the striped pattern into the side stitches for the larger sizes.

The stitches in italics are "action" stitches, and are so marked for ease of following the pattern.

Slip the stitch markers when working across the rows.

GILET
Using Size 6 needles, cast on 231(243, 255) sts.
Row 1 (RS) * K1, P1; rep from * to last st, K1.
Row 2 Purl.
Rows 3–8 Repeat rows 1 and 2 three times. 231(243, 255) sts.
Row 9 (RS) K2, sl2wyib, K2, [K3, yo, K2tog, K5] 5 times, _K0(3, 6), K1 and PM on this stitch, K0(3, 6)_, yo, K2tog, K8, yo, K2tog, K6, sl2wyib, K4, yo, K3, K2tog, [K4, yo, K1, yo, K3, K2tog] 6 times, K4, yo, K4, sl2wyib, K6, yo, K2tog, K8, yo, K2tog, _K0(3, 6), K1 and PM on this stitch, K0(3, 6)_, [K5, yo, K2tog, K3] 5 times, K2, sl2wyib, K2. 238(250, 262) sts.
Row 10 (shift cable row) P2, sl2wyif P2, [P8, yo, P2tog] 5 times, _P1(7, 13)_, P5, yo, P2tog, P9, _yo_, P2, sl2wyif, P2, _P2tog_, P4, [P2tog, P9] 6 times, _P2tog_, P4, P2tog, P2, sl2wyif, P2, _yo_, P9, yo, P2tog, P5, _P1(7, 13)_, [yo, P2tog, P8] 5 times, P2, sl2wyif, P2. 231(243, 255) sts.

Row 11 (cable row) *Cable* 6, [K3, K2tog, yo, K5] 5 times, *K1(7, 13)*, K2tog, yo, K8, K2tog, yo, K5, *cable* 6, K2, yo, K2, K2tog, [K3, yo, K3, yo, K2, K2tog] 6 times, K3, yo, K2, *cable* 6, K5, K2tog, yo, K8, K2tog, yo, *K1(7, 13)*, [K5, K2tog, yo, K3] 5 times, *cable* 6. 238(250, 262) sts.

Row 12 P6, [P8, P2tog, yo] 5 times, *P1(7, 13)*, P5, P2tog, yo, P8, P2tog, yo, P11, [P2tog, P9] 6 times, P2tog, P11, P2tog, yo, P8, P2tog, yo, P5, *P1(7, 13)*, [P2tog, yo, P8] 5 times, P6. 231(243, 255) sts.

Row 13 K2, sl2wyib, K2, [K3, yo, K2tog, K5] 5 times, *K1(7, 13)*, yo, K2tog, K8, yo, K2tog, K7, sl2wyib, K5, yo, K1, K2tog, [K2, yo, K5, yo, K1, K2tog] 6 times, K2, yo, K5, sl2wyib, K7, yo, K2tog, K8, yo, K2tog, *K1(7, 13)*, [K5, yo, K2tog, K3] 5 times, K2, sl2wyib, K2. 238(250, 262) sts.

Row 14 (shift cable row) P2, sl2wyif, P2, [P8, yo, P2tog] 5 times, *P1(7, 13)*, P5, yo, P2tog, P8, yo, P2tog, *yo*, P2, sl2wyif, P2, *P2tog*, P3, [P2tog, P9] 6 times, P2tog, P3, *P2tog*, P2, sl2wyif, P2, *yo*, P10, yo, P2tog, P5, *P1(7, 13)*, [yo, P2tog, P8] 5 times, P2, sl2wyif, P2. 231(243, 255) sts.

Row 15 (cable row and decrease row) *Cable* 6, [K3, K2tog, yo, K5] 4 times, K3, K2tog, yo, K3, *K2tog, K1(7, 13), K2tog*, K8, K2tog, yo, K6, *cable* 6, K3, yo, K2tog, [K1, yo, K7, yo, K2tog] 6 times, K1, yo, K3, *cable* 6, K6, K2tog, yo, K8, *K2tog, K1(7, 13), K2tog*, K3, K2tog, yo, K3, [K5, K2tog, yo, K3] 4 times, *cable* 6. 234(246, 258) sts.

Row 16 P6, [P8, P2tog, yo] 4 times, P9, *P1(7, 13)*, P4, P2tog, yo, P8, P2tog, yo, P11, [P2tog, P9] 6 times, P2tog, P11, P2tog, yo, P8, P2tog yo, P4, *P1(7, 13)*, P9 [P2tog, yo, P8] 4 times, P6. 227(239, 251) sts.

Row 17 K2, sl2wyib, K2, [K3, yo, K2tog, K5] 4 times, K3, yo, K2tog, K4, *K1(7, 13)*, K9, yo, K2tog, K8, sl2wyib, K6, [K1, yo, K3, K2tog, K4, yo] 6 times, K7, sl2wyib, K8, yo, K2tog, K9, *K1(7, 13)*, K4, yo, K2tog, K3, [K5, yo, K2tog, K3] 4 times, K2, sl2wyib, K2. 233(245, 257) sts.

Row 18 (shift cable row) P2, sl2wyif, P2, [P8, yo, P2tog] 4 times, P9, *P1(7, 13)*, P4, yo, P2tog, P8, yo, P2tog, P1, yo, P2, sl2wyif, P2, *P2tog*, [P7, P2tog, P2] 6 times, P5, *P2tog*, P2, sl2wyif, P2, yo, P1, yo, P2tog, P8, yo, P2tog, P4, *P1(7, 13)*, P9, [yo, P2tog, P8] 4 times, P2, sl2wyif, P2. 227(239, 251) sts.

Row 19 (cable row) *Cable* 6, [K3, K2tog, yo, K5] 4 times, K3, K2tog, yo, K4, *K1(7, 13)*, K9, K2tog, yo, K7, *cable* 6, K3, [K2, yo, K2, K2tog K3, yo, K1] 6 times, K4, *cable* 6, K7, K2tog, yo, K9, *K1(7, 13)*, K4, K2tog, yo, K3, [K5, K2tog, yo, K3] 4 times, *cable* 6. 233(245, 257) sts.

Row 20 P6, [P8, P2tog, yo] 4 times, P9, *P1(7, 13)*, P4, P2tog, yo, P8, P2tog, yo, P9, [P7, P2tog, P2] 6 times, P14, P2tog, yo, P8, P2tog, yo, P4, *P1(7, 13)*, P9, [P2tog, yo, P8] 4 times, P6. 227(239, 251) sts.

Row 21 K2, sl2wyib, K2, [K3, yo, K2tog, K5] 4 times, K3, yo, K2tog, K4, *K1(7, 13)*, K9, yo, K2tog, K9, sl2wyib, K5, [K3, yo, K1, K2tog, K2, yo, K2], 6 times, K6, sl2wyib, K9, yo, K2tog, K9, *K1(7, 13)*, K4, yo, K2tog, K3, [K5, yo, K2tog, K3] 4 times, K2, sl2wyib, K2. 233(245, 257) sts.

Row 22 (shift cable row and decrease row) P2, sl2wyif, P2, [P8, yo, P2tog] 4 times, P8, *P0(3, 6), sl1wyif, P2tog, psso, P0(3, 6)*, P3, yo, P2tog, P8, yo, P2tog, P2, *yo*, P2, sl2wyif, P2, *P2tog*, [P6, P2tog, P3] 6 times, P3, *P2tog*, P2, sl2wyif, P2, *yo*, P2, yo, P2tog, P8, yo, P2tog, P3, *P0(3, 6), sl1wyif, P2tog, psso, P0(3, 6)*, P8, [yo, P2tog, P8] 4 times, P2, sl2wyif, P2. 223(235, 247) sts.

Row 23 (cable row) *Cable* 6, [K3, K2tog, yo, K5] 4 times, K3, K2tog, yo, K3, *K1(7, 13)*, K8, K2tog, yo, K8, *cable* 6, K2, [K4, yo, K2tog, K1, yo, K3] 6 times, K3, *cable* 6, K8, K2tog, yo, K8, *K1(7, 13)*, K3, K2tog, yo, K3, [K5, K2tog, yo, K3] 4 times, *cable* 6. 229(241, 253) sts.

Row 24 P6, [P8, P2tog, yo] 4 times, P8, *P1(7, 13)*, P3, P2tog, yo, P8, P2tog, yo, P10, [P6, P2tog, P3] 6 times, P13, P2tog, yo, P8, P2tog, yo, P3, *P1(7, 13)*, P8, [P2tog, yo, P8] 4 times, P6. 223(235, 247) sts.

Row 25 K2, sl2wyib, K2, [K3, yo, K2tog, K5] 4 times, K3, yo, K2tog, K3, *K1(7, 13)*, K8, yo, K2tog, K10, sl2wyib, K5, [K4, yo, K1, yo, K3, K2tog] 6 times. K4, sl2wyib, K10, yo, K2tog, K8, *K1(7, 13)*, K3, yo, K2tog, K3, [K5, yo, K2tog, K3] 4 times, K2, sl2wyib, K2. 229(241, 253) sts.

Row 26 (shift cable row) P2, sl2wyif, P2, [P8, yo, P2tog] 4 times, P8, *P1(7, 13)*, P3, yo, P2tog, P8, yo, P2tog, P3, *yo*, P2, sl2wyif, P2, *P2tog*, P1, [P9, P2tog] 6 times, *P2tog*, P2, sl2wyif, *P2*, yo, P3, yo, P2tog, P8, yo, P2tog, P3, *P1(7, 13)*, P8, [yo, P2tog, P8] 4 times, P2, sl2wyif, P2. 223(235, 247) sts.

Row 27 (cable row) *Cable* 6, [K3, K2tog, yo, K5] 4 times, K3, K2tog, yo, K3, *K1(7, 13)*, K8, K2tog, yo, K9, *cable* 6, K2, [K3, yo, K3, yo, K2, K2tog] 6 times, K1, *cable* 6, K9, K2tog, yo, K8, *K1(7, 13)*, K3, K2tog, yo, K3, [K5, K2tog yo, K3] 4 times, *cable* 6. 229(241, 253) sts.

Row 28 P6, [P8, P2tog, yo] 4 times, P8, *P1(7, 13)*, P3, P2tog, yo, P8, yo, P2tog, P12, [P9, P2tog] 6 times, P11, P2tog, yo, P8, P2tog, yo, P3, *P1(7, 13)*, P8, [P2tog, yo, P8] 4 times, P6. 223(235, 247) sts.

Row 29 (decrease row) K2, sl2wyib, K2, [K3, yo, K2tog, K5] 4 times, K3, yo, K2tog, K2, *K0(3, 6), sl1wyib, K2tog, psso, K0(3, 6)*, K7, yo, K2tog, K9, K2, sl2wyib K4, [K2, yo, K5, yo, K1, K2tog] 6 times, K3, sl2wyib, K11, yo, K2tog, K7, *K0(3, 6), sl1wyib, K2tog, psso, K0(3, 6)*, K2, yo, K2tog, K3, [K5, yo, K2tog, K3] 4 times, K2, sl2wyif K2. 225(237, 249) sts.

Row 30 (shift cable row) P2, sl2wyif, P2, [P8, yo, P2tog] 4 times, P7, *P1(7, 13)*, P2, yo, P2tog, P8, yo, P2tog, P4, *yo*, P2, sl2wyif, P2, *P2tog*, [P9, P2tog] 5 times, P9, *P3tog*, P2, sl2wyif, P2, *yo*, P4, yo, P2tog, P8, yo, P2tog, P2, *P1(7, 13)*, P7, [yo, P2tog, P8] 4 times, P2, sl2wyif, P2. 219(231, 243) sts.

Row 31 (cable row) *Cable* 6, [K3, K2tog, yo, K5] 4 times, K3, K2tog, yo, K2, *K1(7, 13)*, K7, K2tog, yo, K8, K2tog, yo, *cable* 6, K1, [K1, yo, K7, yo, K2tog] 6 times, *cable* 6, K2tog, yo, K8, K2tog, yo, K7, *K1(7, 13)*, K2, K2tog, yo, K3, [K5, K2tog, yo, K3] 4 times, *cable* 6. 225(237, 249) sts.

Row 32 P6, [P8, P2tog, yo] 4 times, P7, *P1(7, 13)*, P2, P2tog, yo, P8, P2tog, yo, P12, [P9, P2tog] 6 times, P11, P2tog, yo, P8, P2tog, yo, P2, *P1(7, 13)*, P7, [P2tog, yo, P8] 4 times, P6. 219(231, 243) sts.

Rows 9-32 set the pattern and position of the side shapings.

Maintaining the continuity of the pattern, continue as follows. Read all the instructions carefully before continuing. (The instructions are given individually but all are carried out at the same time.)

Side shapings

Decrease 2 sts on every seventh row on each side of the gilet, using the marker placed on row 9 and the decreases already made as a guide. On RS rows sl1wyib, K2tog, psso. On WS rows sl1wyif, P2tog, psso. Decreases were made on rows 15, 22, and 29.

More deceases are made on rows 36, 43, 50, 57, 64, 71, 78, 85, 36, 43, 50, 57, 64, 71, 78, and 85.

Increase 2 sts on every fourth row on each side of the gilet, using the marker placed on row 9 as a guide.

For all increases, work to the marked stitch, yo, P1, yo.

Increases are made on rows 90, 94, 98, 102, 106, 110, 114, 118, 122, 126, 130, and 134.

BACK DIAMOND-PATTERN PANEL

As the cables shift toward the center back, it will not be possible to work full diamonds. Work half a diamond, with the diamond edge toward the center back and the straight half-diamond edge toward the cable. This will also prevent the diamond pattern interfering with the P2tog decreases to shift the cable.

CABLE SHIFT

The cable on each side of the back diamond pattern panel shifts inward one place by making a yo on the outside of it and a P2tog on the inside on every 4th row.

Cable shifts were made on rows 10, 14, 18, 22, 26, and 30.

Further cable shifts are made on rows 34, 38, 42, 46, 50, 54, 58, 62, 66, 70, 74, 78, 82, 86, 90, 94, 98, 102, 106, 110, 114, 118, 122, 126, 130, 134, 138, 142, 146, and 150.

On row 150 work the decreases inside the cables as sl1wyif, P2tog, psso so that only one stitch remains between the cables.

The cable later shifts outward one place by making a K2tog or P2tog on the outside of it and a yo on the inside.

Cable shifts are made on rows 162–190 except rows 185, 187, and 189.

Rows 162–164 On RS rows work the stitches between the cables as knit stitches. On WS rows work the stitches between the cables as purl stitches.

Row 165 Work the stitches between the cables as yo, K1, [K1, P1] twice, K2, yo.

Row 166 Work the stitches between the cables as yo, P9, yo.

Row 167 Work the stitches between the cables as yo, K1, [K1, P1] 4 times, K2, yo.

Row 168 Work the stitches between the cables as yo, P13, yo.

Continue in patt until row 194 has been worked.

Row 195 Patt to 26 sts before the center stitch, bind off 53 sts, patt to end. 19(21, 23) sts on each side.

BUTTONHOLES

Row 111 (RS) Patt 6, make a buttonhole over 3 stitches as described on pages 84–87, patt to last 10 sts, make second buttonhole, patt to end.

SHAPE FRONT NECK

Decrease one stitch inside the cable edge. On RS rows work K2tog. On WS rows work P2tog.

Decreases are made on rows 114, 117, 121, 124, 128, 131, 135, 138, 142, 145, 149, 152, 156, 159, 163, 166, 170, 173, 177, 180, 184, 187, and 191.

ARMHOLES

36-inch (91cm) size

Row 139 Patt to 4 sts before the first marked center side stitch, bind off 9 sts, patt to 4 sts before the second marked center side stitch, bind off 9 sts, patt to end.

38- and 40-inch (97- and 102cm) sizes

Row 137 Patt to 4(5) sts before the first marked center side stitch, bind off 9(11) sts, patt to 4(5) sts before the second marked center side stitch, bind off 9(11) sts, patt to end.

All sizes

Work on each piece separately.

Shape armholes

Cont in patt decreasing one stitch at armhole edges inside 2 edge stitches. On RS rows work K2tog. On WS rows work P2tog.

38- and 40-inch (97- and 102-cm) sizes

Decreases are made on row 139.

All sizes

Decreases are made on rows 142, 145, 148, 151, 154, 157, 160, 168, 174, and 180.

Fronts

Decreases are made on row 186.

Cont straight in patt until row 195 has been worked. 19(21, 23) sts.

Shoulders

Left back shoulder and right front shoulder

Row 196 Patt 19(21, 23) sts.

Row 197 Patt 13 sts, turn.

Row 198 Sl6wyif, patt 7.

Bind off all stitches purlwise.

Right back shoulder and left front shoulder

Row 196 Patt 13 sts, turn.

Row 197 Sl6wyib, patt 7.

Bind off all stitches knitwise.

SLEEVES

Using Size 6 needles, cast on 74(76, 78) sts.

Row 1 * K1, P1; rep from * to end.

Row 2 Purl.

Row 3 Repeat row 1.

Row 4 P1, yo, purl to last st, yo, P1. 76(78, 80) sts.

Row 5 K1, * K1, P1; rep from * to last st, K1.

Row 6 Purl.

Row 7 Repeat row 5.

Row 8 Purl.

Row 9 K7(8, 9), [yo, K2tog, K8] 3 times, yo, K2tog, [K8, yo, K2tog] 3 times, K7(8, 9).

Row 10 P1, yo, P1(2, 3), [yo, P2tog, P8] 7 times, yo, P2tog, P1, yo, P1(2, 3). 78(80, 82) sts.

Row 11 [K8, K2tog, yo] 7 times, K8.

Row 12 P3, [P2tog, yo, P8] 7 times, P2tog, yo, P3.

Row 13 [K8, yo K2tog] 7 times, K8.

Row 14 P3, [yo, P2tog, P8] 7 times, yo, P2tog, P3.

Continue in pattern as established increasing 1 stitch at both ends on rows 16, 22, 28, and 34. 86(88, 90) sts.

Row 36 Bind off 3(3, 4) sts knitwise, patt to end. 83(85, 86) sts.

Row 37 Bind off 4(4, 5) sts, patt to end. 79(81, 81) sts.

Row 38 P1, P2tog, patt to last 3 sts, P2tog, P1. 77(79, 79) sts.

Row 39 K1, K2tog, patt to last 3 sts, K2tog, K1. 75(77, 77) sts.

Rows 40-51 Repeat rows 38 and 39 six times. 51(53, 53) sts.

Row 52 P1, sl1wyif, P2tog, psso, patt to last 4 sts, sl1wyif, P2tog, psso, P1. 47(49, 49) sts.

Row 53 K1, sl1wyib, K2tog, psso, patt to last 4 sts, sl1wyif, K2tog, psso, K1. 43(45, 45) sts.

Rows 54-62 Repeat rows 52 and 53 four times and row 52 once. 7(9, 9) sts.

Bind off purlwise.

FINISHING

Block each piece following the instructions on page 138 and referring to the yarn label.

Join shoulder seams.

Insert sleeves and join underarm seams.

Insert ribbon through buttonholes.

Now pour yourself a drink!

a stunning yoke of knitted ribbon, with silk, velvet, satin, and vintage lace intertwined in the design, elevates this simple minidress into a true fashion statement. As long as you follow the basic instructions for the shaping and measurements, you can play around with as many yarns as you like in the yoke. Or, make the basic shift in one yarn, ignoring the instructions to swap yarns, and sew on the decoration afterward.

"Maude" Ruffle Dress   Claire Montgomerie

MATERIALS

10(11, 12) 1¾oz (50g) balls Alchemy Synchronicity, shade 76e Citrine (Yarn A)

Approximately 38 yards (35m) Habu Fringe Tape Ribbon, shade Pale Pink (Yarn B)

Pair Size 7 (4.5mm) knitting needles

One Size 7 (4.5mm) circular needle, 32 inches (80cm) long

Set of four Size 7 (4.5mm) double-pointed needles

Stitch holders

Assorted ribbons and/or buttons to decorate

Button to fasten, approximately ⅜ inch (1cm) diameter

MEASUREMENTS

To fit bust

34	36	38 inches
86	91	97cm

Actual size

35	37	39¼ inches
88	94	100cm

Finished length

34½	34½	34½ inches
87	87	87cm

Sleeve seam length

¾	¾	¾ inches
2	2	2cm

GAUGE

21 sts and 30 rows = 4 inches (10cm) square measured over stockinette stitch using Alchemy Synchronicity (Yarn A) and Size 7 needles or the size required to obtain the correct gauge.

ABBREVIATIONS

See page 129.

fur st Fur stitch. Worked on RS rows. Knit the next stitch without letting it drop off the LHN, bring the yarn forward between the needles, pass the yarn around your thumb or a piece of cardboard to make a loop approximately ¾ inch (2cm) long (or the desired length), take the yarn back between the needles, knit the stitch on the LHN again, this time completing it and letting it drop off the needle. Pass the first loop of the stitch just knitted (now on the RHN) over the second loop of the stitch just knitted and off the needle to secure stitch.

NOTES

When working with the Habu ribbon, work slowly and evenly—it is very easy to knit through the tape instead of the stitch, snagging the ribbon.

Slip the markers when working the rounds.

When short-row shaping, refer to the wrapping technique on page 133.

Rounds 7 and 8 Knit.

Repeating these 2 rounds forms stockinette stitch.

Next round (decrease round) * Knit to the stitch before the marker, K2tog, PM; rep from * once. 208(218, 228) sts.

Cont in st-st, dec 2 sts on every foll 10th round as established to 186(198, 210) sts.

Cont straight in st-st until work measures 27 inches (69cm) from cast-on edge.

BACK

Divide for back and front

Cont working in rows on straight Size 7 needles for back armhole shaping.

Row 1 (RS) Bind off 3 sts, knit to marker and work on these 90(96, 102) sts for the back. Place rem 93(99, 105) sts on a holder for the front.

Row 2 Bind off 3 sts, purl to end. 87(93, 99) sts.

Cont in st-st.

Bind off 3 sts at beg of next 2 rows. 81(87, 93) sts.

Dec 1 st at both ends of next 3 rows and on 3 foll alt rows 69(75, 81) sts.

Cont straight in st-st until armhole measures 3 inches (7.5cm), ending with a WS row.

Shape neck (keyhole neckline)

Next row (RS) K33(36, 39), bind off 3 sts, K32(35, 39) sts.

Turn and work on second set of 33(36, 39) sts for left back neck.

Leave first set of 33(36, 39) sts on a holder.

Bind off 1 st at neck edge on foll 4 alt rows 29(32, 35) sts.

Cont straight in st-st until armhole measures 5½ inches (14cm), ending with a WS row.

Inc 1 st at neck edge on next row, on 2 foll 4th rows, then on foll 2 alt rows. 34(37, 40) sts.

Cont in st-st until armhole measures 7 inches (18cm), ending with a RS row.

Shape left back shoulder

Bind off 4(5, 6) sts at beg of next row and 5(5, 6) sts at beg of foll alt row. 25(27, 28) sts.

Next row (RS) Bind off 20(21, 22) sts, knit to end. 5(6, 6) sts.

Purl one row.

Bind off rem sts.

Rejoin Yarn A to 33(36, 39) sts left on a holder for right side of back neck.

Work to match left side of back neck, reversing shaping.

WORKING THE RUFFLE

The yoke of the dress is worked in a random pattern, but the exact pattern used for the dress shown here has been written. The type of stitch varies along a row, with knit, purl, and fur stitch all used along some rows to try to show off the ribbon to best effect. It is a mixture of stranding—in which the unused yarn is carried along the back of the work—and intarsia, or twisting, in which separate balls or bobbins of yarn are used for each section of color. (Note that when changing color you must twist the two yarns around each other to prevent a hole.) Because this is not a regular way of working and because a mixture of stitches is used within these sections, a chart has not been written as would happen with stranding or intarsia techniques. The instructions have been written in words. This may take some getting used to, but it also allows for interpretation and experimentation by the knitter.

SKIRT

Using a Size 7 circular needle and Yarn A, cast on 210(220, 230) sts. Join for knitting in the round.

Round 1 PM to mark beg of round, K105(110, 115) sts, PM to mark side stitch, knit to end.

Round 2 Purl.

Repeating these 2 rounds forms garter stitch.

Work 4 more rounds in garter st.

FRONT

With RS facing, rejoin Yarn A to the 93(99, 105) sts left on a holder for the front.

Shape armhole for the dress without ribbon

Cont in st-st.

Bind off 3 sts at beg of next 4 rows. 81(87, 93) sts.

Dec 1 st at both ends of next 3 rows and on 3 foll alt rows 69(75, 81) sts.

Beg with a purl row, work 19 rows straight st-st. 32 rows for armhole worked in all.

Cont as for dress with ribbon, starting at the first row of front neck shaping and using Yarn A throughout.

Shape armhole for the dress with ribbon

Work the armhole shaping at the same time as knitting in the ribbon. Each time the new yarn is added, tie it in as for a stripe or for multicolored knitting, either carrying the unused yarn along the back of the work, or using a different ball for each section, twisting the yarn together at the color change as for intarsia.

Cont in st-st.

Row 1 (RS) Using Yarn A, bind off 3 sts, knit to end. 90(96, 102) sts.

Row 2 Using Yarn A, bind off 3 sts, purl to end. 87(93, 99) sts.

Row 3 Using Yarn A, bind off 3 sts, K25(28, 31), join Yarn B and K1, (fur st 1, K1) 3 times, return to Yarn A and knit to end. 84(90, 96) sts.

Row 4 Using Yarn A, bind off 3 sts, P16(19, 22), change to Yarn B and K15, return to Yarn A and purl to end. 81(87, 93) sts.

Row 5 Using Yarn A, dec 1 st at beg of row, knit to 1 st before Yarn B of previous row, change to Yarn B and K20, return to Yarn A and knit to end, decreasing 1 st at end of row. 79(85, 91) sts.

Row 6 Using Yarn A, dec 1 st at beg of row, purl to first Yarn B st of previous row, change to Yarn B and K25, return to Yarn A and purl to end, decreasing 1 st at end of row. 77(83, 89) sts.

Row 7 Using Yarn A, dec 1 st at beg of row, K28(31, 34), change to Yarn B and K1, (fur st 1, K1) 4 times, return to Yarn A and knit to end, decreasing 1 st at end of row. 75(81, 87) sts.

Row 8 Using Yarn A, purl.

Row 9 Using Yarn A, knit, dec 1 st at both ends of the row. 73(79, 85) sts.

Row 10 Using Yarn A, purl.

Row 11 Using Yarn A, dec 1 st at beg of row, K5(8, 11), change to Yarn B and K14, return to Yarn A and knit to end, decreasing 1 st at end of row. 71(77, 83) sts.

Row 12 Using Yarn A, purl to 1 st before Yarn B of previous row, change to Yarn B and K16, return to Yarn A and purl to end of row.

Row 13 Using Yarn A, dec 1 st at beg of row, K8(11, 14), change to Yarn B and K10, return to Yarn A and knit to end of row, decreasing 1 st at end of row 69(75, 81) sts.

Rows 14-16 Using Yarn A, work 3 rows straight in st-st.

Row 17 Using Yarn A, K20(23, 26), change to Yarn B and K5, (fur st 1, K1) 10 times, K5, return to Yarn A and knit to end.

Row 18 Using Yarn A, purl to where Yarn B begins on previous row, change to Yarn B and K31, return to Yarn A and purl to end.

Row 19 Using Yarn A, knit.

Row 20 Using Yarn A, purl to 2 sts before Yarn B begins on row 18, change to Yarn B and K35, return to Yarn A and purl to end.

Rows 21-24 Using Yarn A, beg with a knit row work 4 rows st-st.

Row 25 Using Yarn A, K28(31, 34), change to Yarn B and K1, (fur st 1, K1) 3 times, (fur st 1, K2) 5 times, return to Yarn A and knit to end.

Row 26 Using Yarn A, purl to 3 sts before Yarn B begins on previous row, change to Yarn B and K28, return to Yarn A and purl to end.

Row 27 Using Yarn A, knit.

Row 28 Using Yarn A, purl to 3 sts before Yarn B begins on previous row, change to Yarn B and K33, return to Yarn A and purl to end.

Rows 29 and 30 Using Yarn A, work 2 rows st-st.

Row 31 Using Yarn A, K5(8, 11), change to Yarn B and K1, (fur st 1, K1) 4 times, return to Yarn A and knit to end.

Row 32 Using Yarn A, P8(11, 14), change to Yarn B and K32, return to Yarn A and purl to end.

Shape front neck

Row 1 (RS) Using Yarn A, K23(25, 27), bind off 23(25, 27) sts for center front neck, knit to end. Turn and work on this second set of 23(25, 27) sts for right side of front neck. Leave first set of 23(25, 27) sts on a holder for left side of front neck.

Row 2 (WS) Using Yarn B, knit.

Row 3 Using Yarn A, bind off 4(5, 6) sts, knit to end. 19(20, 21) sts.

Row 4 Using Yarn B, knit to end, dec 1 st at neck edge. 18(19, 20) sts.

Row 5 Using Yarn A, knit to end dec 1 st at neck edge. 17(18, 19) sts.

Row 6 Using Yarn A, purl to end, dec 1 st at neck edge. 16(17, 18) sts.

Row 7 Using Yarn A, K4(5, 6), change to Yarn B, K1 (fur st 1, K1) twice, change to Yarn A and knit to end.

Row 8 Using Yarn A, purl, dec 1 st at neck edge. 15(16, 17) sts.

Row 9 Using Yarn A, knit.

Row 10 Using Yarn B, knit, dec 1 st at neck edge. 14(15, 16) sts.

Cut Yarn B.

Using Yarn A, cont in st-st until armhole measures 7(7½, 8) inches/ 18(19, 20)cm to shoulder shaping, ending with a RS row.

Shape shoulder

Bind off 4(5, 6) sts at beg of next row and 5 sts at beg of foll alt row. 5(5, 5) sts.

Next row (RS) Knit.
Bind off rem 5 sts.

Rejoin Yarn A to K23(25, 27) sts left on a holder for left front neck. Work to match right side of front neck, reversing shaping and working Yarn B as desired.

CAP SLEEVES (Make 2)

Block each piece following the instructions on page 138 and referring to the yarn label. Do not press the ruffled area.
Join shoulder seams.
With RS facing, using Yarn A and Size 7 straight needles, pick up 38(40, 42) sts evenly along armhole edge from start of armhole shaping excluding the bound-off sts, over the shoulder and to end of armhole shaping excluding the bound-off sts.
Work the cap sleeves in short-shaping rows (see page 133).
P34(36, 38), turn, leaving rem unworked sts on needle.
K30(32, 34), turn.
P26(28, 30), turn.
K22(24, 26), turn.
P18(20, 22), turn.
K14(16, 18), turn.
P10(12, 14), turn.
K6(8, 10), turn.
P10(12, 14), working back across sts left on needle, turn.
K14(16, 18), turn.
P18(20, 22), turn.
K22(24, 26), turn.
P26(28, 30), turn.
K30(32, 34), turn.
Purl back across all 38(40, 42) sts

Transfer these 38(40, 42) sts onto Size 7 double-pointed needles. Change to Yarn B and knit across the 38(40, 42) sts, pick up and knit 22 sts from underarm and join for working in the round. 60(62, 64) sts.
Purl one row.
Bind off all sts.

NECKBAND

Using a Size 7 circular needle and Yarn B, cast on 4 sts. With RS of dress facing and using the needle with the cast-on sts, pick up and knit one stitch in every stitch around the neck, cast on 4 sts.
Row 1 Do not join in a round. Turn and knit across all stitches.
Bind off all stitches.

FINISHING

Join side and sleeve seams.
Sew the fastening button to the back of the neck. The ribbon should have sufficient gaps to allow for a button to pass through without the need to make a buttonhole.
Attach additional ribbon and buttons to the ruffled yoke if desired.

This pretty sweater is knitted in stockinette stitch in a soft, silk-and-wool-blend yarn, with a fringe of shimmering nylon tape at the neck and cuffs. This is a great way to use ribbon, tape, or other fancy yarns that may not be suitable for knitting an entire garment. Fur stitch is a good way to show off the qualities of a more unusual yarn, such as this tape's natural drape.

"Babs" Fringed Jumper Claire Montgomerie

MATERIALS
5(6, 7) 1¾oz (50g) balls Louisa Harding Grace, shade 04 Pink (Yarn A)
1(1, 1) 1¾oz (50g) ball Louisa Harding Fauve, shade 19 Beige (Yarn B)
One Size 7 (4.5mm) circular needle, 32 inches (80cm) long
Pair Size 7 (4.5mm) knitting needles
Button to fasten, approximately ⅜ inch (1cm) diameter

MEASUREMENTS
To fit bust

34	36	38 inches
86	91	97cm

Actual size

35	37½	39¾ inches
89	95	101cm

Length

21	22½	23½ inches
54	57	60cm

Sleeve seam length

10¼	11	11¾ inches
26	28	30cm

GAUGE
21 sts and 30 rows = 4 inches (10cm) square over stockinette stitch using Grace (Yarn A) and Size 7 (4.5mm) needles or the size required to obtain the correct gauge.

ABBREVIATIONS
See page 129.
fur st Fur stitch. Worked on RS rows. Knit the next stitch without letting it drop off the LHN, bring the yarn forward between the needles, pass the yarn around your thumb or a piece of cardboard to make a loop approximately ¾ inch (2cm) long (or the desired length), take the yarn back between the needles, knit the stitch on the LHN again, this time completing it and letting it drop off the needle. Pass

the first loop of the stitch just knitted (now on the RHN) over the second loop of the stitch just knitted and off the needle to secure stitch.

NOTES
Slip the markers when working the rounds, unless otherwise stated.

BODY
Using a Size 7 circular needle and Yarn A, cast on 206(218, 230) sts. Join for knitting in the round.
Round 1 PM to mark beg of round, K103(109, 115) sts, PM to mark side stitch, knit to end.
Round 2 Purl.
Repeating these 2 rounds forms garter stitch.
Work 4 more rounds in garter st.

Rounds 7 and 8 Knit.
Repeating these 2 round forms st-st.
Round 9 (decrease round) * Knit to st before marker, K2tog, PM; rep from * once. 204(216, 228) sts.
Cont in st-st, dec 2 sts on every foll 10th round as established to 188(200, 212) sts.
Cont straight in st-st until work measures 14(15, 15¾) inches/36(38, 40)cm from cast-on edge.

FRONT
Divide for back and front
Row 1 Bind off 5 sts, knit to marker, place next 94(100, 106) sts on holder for the back and work on rem 89(95, 101) sts.
Row 2 Bind off 5 sts, purl to end. 84(90, 96) sts.
Cont in st-st, binding off 3 sts at beg of next 2 rows. 78(84, 90) sts.
Dec 1 st at both ends of next 3 rows and on 3 foll alt rows. 66(72, 78) sts.
Work 5(7, 9) rows in st-st, beg and ending with a purl row.
Next row (RS) Join Yarn B and begin working the intarsia pattern, following the chart, starting the first stitch of the chart on the

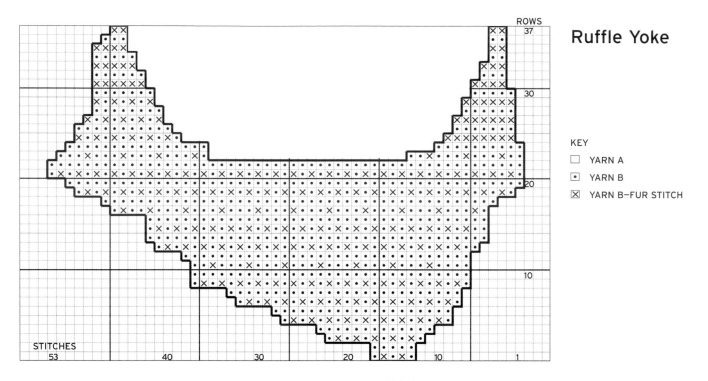

ROWS
37
30
20
10

STITCHES
53　40　30　20　10　1

Ruffle Yoke

KEY
☐ YARN A
⊡ YARN B
☒ YARN B—FUR STITCH

10th(13th, 16th) stitch of the row. The first Yarn B stitch on this row is the 13th stitch of the chart [the 22nd(25th, 28th) stitch of the row]. Work until armhole measures 5(5½, 6) inches/13(14, 15)cm, ending with a WS row.

Shape neck

Row 1 Continuing and maintaining the intarsia pattern, K22(25, 28) sts, bind off 22 sts, knit to end.

Turn and work on this second set of 22(25, 28) sts for right side of front neck. Leave the first set of sts on a holder for left side of front neck.

Next row Patt.

Next row Bind off 3 sts, patt to end. 19(22, 25) sts.

Dec 1 st at neck edge on next 2 rows and 4 foll alt rows 13(16, 19) sts.

Cont in patt until armhole measures 7(7½, 8) inches/18(19, 20)cm, ending with a RS row.

Shape shoulder

Bind off 4(5, 5) sts at beg of next and foll alt row. 5(6, 9) sts.

Bind off rem sts.

Rejoin Yarns B and A to the 22(25, 28) sts left on a holder for the left side of front neck.

Work to match right side of front neck, reversing shaping.

BACK

Rejoin Yarn A to the 94(100, 106) sts on the holder.

Cont in st-st, bind off 5 sts at beg of next 2 rows, and 3 sts at beg of foll 2 rows. 78(84, 90) sts.

Dec 1 st at both ends of next 3 rows and 3 foll alt rows 66(72, 78) sts.

Cont in st-st without shaping until armhole measures 3(3½, 4) inches/8(9, 10)cm, ending with a WS row.

Shape neck

Next row K31(34, 37), bind off 4 sts, K30(33, 36). Turn and work on this second set of 31(34, 37) sts for left back neck. Leave first set of sts on a holder for right side of back neck

Bind off 1 st at neck edge on next 4 alt rows. 27(30, 33) sts.

Cont in st-st without shaping until armhole measures 5½(6, 6¼) inches/14(15, 16)cm, ending with a WS row.

Inc 1 st at neck edge on the next row, foll 4th row, then on 4 foll alt rows. 33(36, 39) sts.

Cont straight in st-st without shaping until armhole measures 7(7½, 8) inches/14(15, 16)cm, ending with a RS row.

Shape shoulder

Bind off 4(5, 5) sts at beg of next row and foll alt row. 25(26, 29) sts.

Next row (RS) Bind off 16(17, 18) sts, knit to end. 9(9, 11) sts.

Purl one row.

Bind off 4(4, 5) sts at beg of next row, knit to end. 5(5, 6) sts.

Bind off rem sts.

Rejoin Yarn A to 31(34, 37) sts left on a holder for the right side
of back neck.
Work to match left side of back neck, reversing shaping.

SLEEVES
Using a Size 7 circular needle and Yarn B, cast on 52(54, 56) sts.
Row 1 K1, * fur st 1, K1; rep from * to last st, K1.
Row 2 Knit.
Row 3 K2, * fur st 1, K1; rep from * to end.
Cut Yarn B.
Join Yarn A.
Row 4 Purl.
Work 4 more rows in st-st, ending with a WS row.
Cont in st-st, inc 1 st at both ends of next row and every foll twelfth
row to 62(66, 68) sts. Cont straight in st-st without shaping until
sleeve measures 10¼(11, 11¾) inches/26(28, 30)cm from cast-on edge.

Shape sleeve top
Bind off 5 sts at beg of next 2 rows. 52(56, 58) sts.
Bind off 3 sts at beg of foll 2 rows. 46(50, 52) sts.
Dec 1 st at both ends of next 3 rows and 2 foll alt rows 36(40, 42) sts.
Work 3(3, 5) rows.
Dec 1 at both ends of next row and 4 foll 4th rows. 26(30, 32) sts.
Work 1(3, 5) rows.
Dec 1 st at both ends of next row and foll alt row, then on every row
until 18(20, 22) sts rem, ending with a WS row.
Bind off 3 sts at beg of next 4 rows. 6(8, 10) sts.
Bind off rem 6(8, 10) sts.

FINISHING
Block each piece following the instructions on page 138 and referring
to the yarn label.
Join shoulder seams and sew in sleeves.
Join side and sleeve seams.

NECK EDGING
Using a Size 7 circular needle and Yarn A, cast on 4 sts. With RS of
sweater facing and using the needle with the cast-on sts, pick up
20(21, 22) sts along left back neck, 14(15, 16) sts along left front neck,
22 sts from bound-off edge of front neck, 14(15, 16) sts along right front
neck, 20(21, 22) sts from right back neck, cast on 4 sts. 98(102, 106) sts.
Work 2 rows garter st.
Next row (buttonhole row) K2, yo, K2tog, knit to end.
Knit one row.
Bind off knitwise (on WS).
Sew on button to correspond with buttonhole.

This simple silky-knit tunic dress with wide butterfly sleeves is actually much easier to knit than it looks and can be made as long or as short as you wish (to wear by itself or over jeans). We love the Missoni-esque pattern of graduating chevron stripes, and the wonderful choice of yarns makes it slinky and shimmery, draping in all the right places.

"Mae" Tunic Dress Louisa Harding

MATERIALS

4(4, 5, 5) 1¾oz (50g) balls Louisa Harding Glisten, shade 2 Silver (Yarn A)
3(3, 4, 4) 1¾oz (50g) balls Louisa Harding Impression, shade 10 Blue (Yarn B)
1(2, 2, 2) 1oz (25g) balls Louisa Harding Kashmir Aran Pure, shade 6 Teal (Yarn C)
2(2, 3, 3) 1¾oz (50g) balls Louisa Harding Grace, shade 8 Purple (Yarn D)
2(3, 3, 4) 1¾oz (50g) balls Louisa Harding Impression, shade 11 Slate (Yarn E)
3(3, 4, 4) 1¾oz (50g) balls Louisa Harding Grace, shade 3 Dove (Yarn F)
Pair each Size 6 (4mm) and 7 (4.5mm) knitting needles
Row counter

MEASUREMENTS

To fit bust

30-32	34-36	38-40	42-44 inches
76-81	86-91	97-102	107-112cm

Actual size

36	41	45	49½ inches
92	104	114	126cm

Finished length

32	32	32	32 inches
81.5	81.5	81.5	81.5cm

Sleeve seam length

12	12	12	12 inches
30.5	30.5	30.5	30.5cm

GAUGE

23 sts and 26 rows = 4 inches/10cm square measured over chevron pattern using Size 7 needles or the size required to obtain the correct gauge.

ABBREVIATIONS

See page 129.

BACK AND FRONT (Make 2)

Using Size 7 needles and Yarn A, cast on 138(155, 172, 189) sts.

Row 1 (Edging row 1) (decrease row) (RS) K1, [K2tog, K13, K2tog tbl] 8(9, 10, 11) times, K1. 122(137, 152, 167) sts.
Row 2 (Edging row 2) (WS) Knit.
Cut Yarn A.

Join Yarn B.

Row 3 (Edging row 3) (decrease row) (RS) K1, [K2tog, K11, K2tog tbl] 8(9, 10, 11) times, K1. 106(119, 132, 145) sts.
Row 4 (Edging row 4) (WS) Knit.
Cut Yarn B.

Join Yarn C.

Row 5 (Chevron Edging row 1) (RS) K1, [K2tog, K4, M1, K1, M1, K4, K2tog tbl] 8(9, 10, 11) times, K1. 106(119, 132, 145) sts.
Row 6 (Chevron Edging row 2) (WS) Knit.
Repeating these 2 rows forms chevron edging pattern.

Rows 7-12 Work chevron edging pattern in stripe sequence as follows:
2 rows Yarn D,
2 rows Yarn B,
2 rows Yarn E.
Cut Yarn E.

Join Yarn F.

Row (Chevron row 1) (RS) K1, [K2tog, K4, M1, K1, M1, K4, K2tog tbl] 8(9, 10, 11) times, K1. 106(119, 132, 145) sts.
Row 14 (Chevron row 2) (WS) K1, P to last st, K1.
Repeating these 2 rows forms chevron pattern.

Continue in chevron pattern following the written instructions as follows or following the stripe sequence from the chart on page 48, starting at row 15 until the row 200 is completed or work measures 30 inches (77cm), ending with a WS row.

Stripe Sequence

KEY

□	A	■	D
⊙	B	⊠	E
●	C	⊡	F

Rows 15-34 Work chevron pattern in stripe sequence
as follows:
2 rows Yarn A,
2 rows Yarn D,
2 rows Yarn E.
Rows 21 and 22 2 rows Yarn F,
2 rows Yarn A,
2 rows Yarn B,
2 rows Yarn C,
2 rows Yarn D,
2 rows Yarn B,
2 rows Yarn E.

Rows 35-100 Repeat rows 13-34 three times.
Rows 101-142 Repeat rows 21-34 three times.
Rows 143-150 Work chevron pattern in stripe sequence
as follows:
2 rows Yarn F,
2 rows Yarn A,
2 rows Yarn B,
2 rows Yarn E.
Rows 151-174 Repeat rows 143-150 three times.
Rows 175-180 Work chevron pattern in stripe sequence
as follows:
2 rows Yarn F,
2 rows Yarn A,
2 rows Yarn E.
Rows 181-198 Repeat rows 175-180 three times.
Rows 199-200 Work chevron pattern in Yarn F.
Work should measure 30 inches (77cm). If necessary, continue to
work in chevron pattern and stripe sequence until work measures
30 inches (77cm), ending with a WS row.
Cut yarn.

Neck edging
Join Yarn A.
Next row (decrease row) (RS) K1, [K2tog, K9, K2tog tbl] 8(9, 10, 11)
times, K1. 90(101, 112, 123) sts.
Next row (WS) Purl.

Change to Size 6 needles and work 11 rows in garter st in the
following stripe sequence:
2 rows Yarn D,
2 rows Yarn E,
2 rows Yarn F,
2 rows Yarn A,

2 rows Yarn D,
1 row Yarn B.
Using Yarn B, bind off knitwise on WS.

SLEEVES (Make 2)
Using Size 7 needles and Yarn A, cast on 121 sts.
Row 1 (Edging row 1) (decrease row) (RS) K1, (K2tog, K13, K2tog tbl)
7 times, K1. 107 sts.
Row 2 (Edging row 2) (WS) Knit.
Cut Yarn A.

Join Yarn B.
Row 3 (Edging row 3) (decrease row) (RS) K1, (K2tog, K11, K2tog tbl)
7 times, K1. 93 sts.
Row 4 (Edging row 4) (WS) Knit.
Cut Yarn B.

Join Yarn C.
Row 5 (Chevron Edging row 1) (RS) K1, (K2tog, K4, M1, K1, M1, K4,
K2tog tbl) 7 times, K1. 93 sts.
Row 6 (Chevron Edging row 2) (WS) Knit.
Repeating these 2 rows forms chevron edging pattern.

Rows 7–10 Work chevron edging pattern in stripe sequence
as follows:
2 rows Yarn D,
2 rows Yarn B.

Cut Yarn B.
Join Yarn E.
Row 11 (Chevron row 1) (RS) K1, [K2tog, K4, M1, K1, M1, K4, K2tog tbl]
7 times, K1. 93 sts.
Row 12 (Chevron row 2 (WS) K1, P to last st, K1.
These 2 rows form the chevron pattern.

Cont in chevron pattern following the stripe sequence as for the
front and back, starting at row 101 and working until sleeve measures
12 inches (30cm), ending with a WS row.

Join Yarn A.
Next row (decrease row) (RS) K1, [K2tog, K9, K2tog tbl] 7 times, K1.
79 sts.
Next row K1, P to last st, K1.
Next row Knit.
Bind off knitwise on WS.

FINISHING
Block each piece following the instructions on page 138 and referring
to the yarn label.
Join shoulder seams, leaving 10½ inches (27cm) open for the neck.
Place markers along the side edges of the front and back 8 inches
(20.5cm) on either side of shoulder seam.
Place center of bound-off edge of sleeves to shoulder seams, then
sew sleeves to back and front between markers.
Join side and sleeve seams.

the wide neckline of this romantic lace-stitch chevron top has a pretty
picot bind-off and a sweet flower closure, which make it ultra-feminine.
The fit around the body is relaxed and slouchy, while the wide sleeves are
pulled in tight with deep ribbed cuffs. The subtle shades of cream, butter,
and rose give this gorgeous garment a sense of timeless elegance.

"Edith" Chevron Top   Louisa Harding

MATERIALS

4(4, 5, 5) 1¾oz (50g) balls Louisa Harding Grace, shade 2 Soft Gold (Yarn A)

2(2, 2, 2) 1¾oz (50g) balls Louisa Harding Impression, shade 12
  Vanilla (Yarn B)

2(3, 3, 3) 1¾oz (50g) balls Louisa Harding Kimono Ribbon Pure,
  shade 1 Rice (Yarn C)

3(3, 3, 4) 1¾oz (50g) balls Louisa Harding Grace, shade 4 Rose (Yarn D)

1(2, 2, 3) 1¾oz (50g) balls Louisa Harding Glisten, shade 23 Crème (Yarn E)

Pair each Size 5 (3.75mm), 6 (4mm) and 7 (4.5mm) knitting needles

MEASUREMENTS

To fit bust

30-32	34-36	38-40	42-44 inches
76-81	86-91	97-102	107-112cm

Actual size

38	42	47	51 inches
96	107	119	130cm

Finished length

20	21	22	23 inches
51	53.5	56	58.5cm

Sleeve seam length

13	13	13	13 inches
33	33	33	33cm

GAUGE

24 sts and 24 rows = 4 inches (10cm) square measured over lace
chevron pattern using Size 7 needles or the size required to obtain
the correct gauge.

ABBREVIATIONS

See page 129.

BACK AND FRONT (Make 2)

Using Size 7 needles and Yarn A, cast on 115(129, 143, 157) sts.

Edging row 1 (RS) K1, K2tog, [K5, yo, K1, yo, K5, sl1, K2tog, psso]
7(8, 9, 10) times, K5, yo, K1, yo, K5, skpo, K1.

Edging row 2 Knit.

These two rows form the edging pattern.

Work 4 more rows in patt.

Cut Yarn A.

Join Yarn B.

Lace Chevron row 1 (RS) K1, K2tog, [K5, yo, K1, yo, K5, sl1, K2tog,
psso] 7(8, 9, 10) times, K5, yo, K1, yo, K5, skpo, K1.

Lace Chevron row 2 K1, P to last st, K1.

Repeating rows 1 and 2 forms the lace chevron pattern.

Cut Yarn B.

Join Yarn C and work 2 rows lace chevron pattern.

Continue to work in lace chevron patt working 20 row stripe patt
as follows:

2 rows Yarn A,

2 rows Yarn D,

2 rows Yarn A,

2 rows Yarn C,

2 rows Yarn B,

2 rows Yarn D,

2 rows Yarn E,

2 rows Yarn D,

2 rows Yarn B,

2 rows Yarn C.

Cont in lace chevron patt and stripe sequence until work measures
18½(19½, 20½, 21½) inches/47(49.5, 52, 54.5)cm, ending with a WS row.

Cut yarn.

Join Yarn A and work top edging.

Next row (decrease row) (RS) K1, K2tog, [K11, sl1, K2tog, psso] 7(8, 9, 10) times, K11, skpo, K1. 99(111, 123, 135) sts.
Next row K1, P to last st, K1.
Cut Yarn A.

Change to Size 6 needles, join Yarn D and work 2 rows in garter st.
Change to Yarn A and work 2 rows in garter st.
Change to Yarn C and work 3 rows in garter st.
Next row (WS) K1, P1, * yo, P2tog; rep from * to last st, K1.
99(111, 123, 135) sts.
Work 2 rows in garter st.
Change to Yarn B and work 2 rows in garter st.
Change to Yarn D and work 2 rows in garter st.
Change to Yarn E and knit 1 row.

Using Yarn E, bind off 21(27, 33, 39) sts, then work picot bind-off as follows [slip st on RHN back onto LHN, cast on 2 sts, then bind off 5 sts] 19 times, then bind off to end.

SLEEVES (Make 2)
Using Size 5 needles and Yarn A, cast on 80 sts.
Row 1 (RS) * K1, P1, rep from * to end.
Row 2 (WS) * K1, P1; rep from * to end.
Repeating rows 1 and 2 forms rib
Cont in rib until sleeve measures 5 inches (13cm) from cast-on edge, ending with a RS row.
Next row (Increase row) (WS) [Rib 4, M1, rib 3, M1] 10 times, rib 4, M1, rib 6. 101 sts.

Change to Size 7 needles.
Next row (RS) Knit.
Next row K1, purl to last st, K1.
Cut Yarn A.

Join Yarn B.
Lace Chevron row 1 (RS) K1, K2tog, [K5, yo, K1, yo, K5, sl1, K2tog, psso] 6 times, K5, yo, K1, yo, K5, skpo, K1.
Lace Chevron row 2 K1, P to last st, K1.

Repeating rows 1 and 2 forms the lace chevron pattern.
Cut Yarn B.

Join Yarn C and work 2 rows lace chevron patt.
Continue to work in lace chevron patt working 20 row stripe patt as follows:
2 rows Yarn A,
2 rows Yarn D,
2 rows Yarn A,
2 rows Yarn C,
2 rows Yarn B,
2 rows Yarn D,
2 rows Yarn E,
2 rows Yarn D,
2 rows Yarn B,
2 rows Yarn C.
Cont in lace chevron patt and stripe sequence until sleeve measures 13 inches (33cm) from cast-on edge, ending with a WS row.
Cut yarn.

Join Yarn A.
Next row (decrease row) (RS) K1, K2tog, [K11, sl1, K2tog, psso] 6 times, K11, skpo, K1. 87 sts.
Next row K1, P to last st, K1.
Next row Knit.
Bind off knitwise on WS.

FINISHING
Block each piece following the instructions on page 138 and referring to the yarn label.
Join shoulder seams, leaving the picot edge bind-off open for the neck.
Place markers along side edges of front and back 8½ inches (21cm) on either side of shoulder seams.
Place center of bound-off edge of sleeves to shoulder seams, then sew sleeves to back and front between markers.
Join side and sleeve seams.
Starting at right back shoulder edge, thread two strands of Yarn C through eyelets in top edging of back and secure in place.
Starting at right front shoulder edge, thread two strands of Yarn C through eyelets in top edging of front and secure in place.

SMALL FLOWERS (Make 3)
Using Size 7 needles and Yarn C, cast on 36 sts.
Row 1 * K1, bind off 4 sts (2 sts on RHN), rep from * to end. 12 sts.
Thread yarn through rem sts, pull tight and secure.
Arrange flowers on shoulder edging where ribbons meet at start of left front neck opening and sew in place using photograph as a guide.
Secure lengths of Yarn C at base of flowers to hang down like ribbons.
Cut lengths at a slanted angle to prevent fraying.
If desired, embroider French knots (see page 137) in the center of each flower using Yarn C, and after securing let the tails hang down as ribbons.

divine
accessories

airylike billows of Rowan Kidsilk Haze are fashioned into a feather-light scarf or wrap using three lace patterns: knot stitch, crossed eyelet stitch, and a swirl border. Perfect for an intermediate knitter who wants to try lacework, this delicate, weblike design works up quickly and uses only a few balls of luxurious yarn, though it can be made to any desired length or width.

"Anisette" Wrap

Kristeen Griffin-Grimes for French Girl

MATERIALS
1(2) 1¾oz (50g) balls Rowan Kidsilk Haze, shade 590 Pearl
Pair Size 10 (6mm) knitting needles
One Size 9 (5.5mm) circular needle (sharp-pointed for lacework), 24 inches (60cm) long
Stitch markers
Row counter

MEASUREMENTS
Scarf approximately 11 inches (28cm) wide, length adjustable

Wrap approximately 30 x 60 inches (76 x 142cm) blocked

GAUGE
12 sts and 16 rows = 3 x 3½ inches (7.5 x 8.75cm) over unblocked knot-stitch pattern using a Size 9 circular needle or the size required to obtain the correct gauge.

ABBREVIATIONS
See page 129.
C4B Place RHN needle in front of first 2 sts on LHN, insert RHN into front of next 2 sts on LHN from right to left. Slide all 4 sts off LHN, keeping original 2 sts on RHN and slipping first 2 sts off LHN. Place the loose 2 sts back on LHN, then replace the pair of sts from RHN, thereby crossing them over the sts already on LHN. Knit these 4 sts.

NOTES
The first set of figures refers to the scarf while the figures in parentheses ( ) refer to the wrap. Where only one figure is given, this applies to both the scarf and the wrap.

The number of stitches changes over the rows.

Slip the markers when working across the rows.

KNOT-STITCH SAMPLE SWATCH
Cast on a multiple of 3 sts (12 sts are used for this sample swatch).
Row 1 (RS) Knit.
Row 2 K2, * yo, K3, then use the tip of LHN to lift the first knit stitch of the 3 sts just worked over the last two knit sts; rep from * to last st, K1.
Row 3 Knit.

Row 4 K1, * K3, then use the tip of LHN to lift the first knit stitch of the 3 sts just worked over the last two knit sts, yo; rep from * to last 2 sts, K2. These four rows form the knot-stitch pattern.

SCARF AND WRAP

Using Size 10 needles and the cable method (see pages 133–34), cast on 13 sts for swirl border, PM, 12(60) sts for center panel of scarf (wrap), PM, 13 sts for swirl border. 38(86) sts for scarf (wrap).

Change to Size 9 circular needle and work back and forth.

Row 1 (RS) Sl1P, K1, yo, K2tog, yo, K5, yo, K4, SM, K12(60), SM, K4, yo, K5, yo, K2tog, yo, K2. 42(90) sts.

Row 2 (WS) Sl1P, K1, purl to marker, SM, K2, * yo, K3, then use the tip of LHN to lift the first knit st of the 3 sts just worked over the last two knit sts; rep from * to last st before marker, K1, SM, purl to last 2 sts, K2.

Row 3 Sl1P, [K2tog, yo] twice, K2, sl1, K2tog, psso, K5, SM, knit to marker, SM, K5, sl1, K2tog, psso, K2, [yo, K2tog] twice, K1. 38(86) sts.

Row 4 Sl1P, K1, purl to marker, SM, K1, * K3, then use the tip of LHN to lift the first knit stitch of the 3 sts just worked over the last 2 knit sts, yo; rep from * to last 2 sts before marker, K2, SM, purl to last 2 sts, K2.

Row 5 Sl1P, [K2tog, yo] twice, K2, skpo, K4, SM, knit to marker, SM, K4, skpo, K2, [yo, K2tog] twice, K1. 36(84) sts.

Rows 6, 10, 14, 18, 22, and 26 Repeat row 2.

Row 7 Sl1P, [K2tog, yo] twice, K2, skpo, K3, SM, knit to marker, SM, K3, skpo, K2, [yo, K2tog] twice, K1. 34(82) sts.

Rows 8, 12, 16, 20, and 24 Repeat row 4.

Row 9 Sl1P, [K2tog, yo] twice, K2, skpo, K2, SM, knit to marker, SM, K2, skpo, K2, [yo, K2tog] twice, K1. 32(80) sts.

Row 11 Sl1P, K1, yo, K2tog, yo, K1, yo, K2, skpo, K1, SM, knit to marker, SM, K1, skpo, K2, yo, K1, yo, K2tog, yo, K2. 34(82) sts.

Row 13 Sl1P, K1, yo, K2tog, [yo, K3] twice, K1, SM, knit to marker, SM, K1, [K3, yo] twice, K2tog, yo, K2. 38(86) sts.

Row 15 Repeat row 1.

Row 17 Repeat row 3.

Row 19 Repeat row 5.

Row 21 Repeat row 7.

Row 23 Repeat row 9.

Row 25 Repeat row 11.

Row 27 Repeat row 13.

FOR THE SCARF ONLY

Row 28 Repeat row 14.

Continue repeating rows 1–28 until desired length is reached, ending with a fourteenth row or a twenty-eighth row. Using Size 10 needles, bind off loosely as given for the wrap.

FOR THE WRAP ONLY

Change to crossed eyelet stitch.

Row 28 and every foll alt row (WS) Sl1P, K1, purl to marker, SM, * K1, P8, K1; repeat from * 5 times, SM, purl to last 2 sts, K2.

Row 29 (RS) Sl1P, K1, yo, K2tog, yo, K5, yo, K4, SM, * P1, K8, P1, repeat from * 5 times, SM, K4, yo, K5, yo, K2tog, yo, K2. 90 sts.

Row 31 Sl1P, [K2tog, yo] twice, K2, sl1, K2tog, psso, K5, SM, * P1, K1, [skpo, yo] 3 times, K1, P1, repeat from * 5 times, SM, K5, sl1, K2tog, psso, K2, [yo, K2tog] twice, K1. 86 sts.

Row 33 Sl1P, [K2tog, yo] twice, K2, skpo, K4, SM, * P1, K1, [skpo, yo] 3 times, K1, P1, repeat from * 5 times, SM, K4, skpo, K2, [yo, K2tog] twice, K1. 84 sts.

Row 35 Sl1P, [K2tog, yo] twice, K2, skpo, K3, SM, * P1, [skpo, yo] 3 times, K2, P1, repeat from * 5 times, SM, K3, skpo, K2, [yo, K2tog] twice, K1. 82 sts.

Row 37 Sl1P, [K2tog, yo] twice, K2, skpo, K2, SM, * P1, K1, [skpo, yo] twice, K3, P1, repeat from * 5 times, SM, K2, skpo, K2, [yo, K2tog] twice, K1. 80 sts.

Row 39 Sl1P, K1, yo, K2tog, yo, K1, yo, K2, skpo, K1, SM, P1, C4B, K4, P1, repeat from * 5 times, SM, K1, skpo, K2, yo, K1, yo, K2tog, yo, K2. 82 sts.

Row 41 Sl1P, K1, yo, K2tog, [yo, K3] twice, K1, SM, * P1, K8, P1, repeat from * to next marker, SM, K1, [K3, yo] twice, K2tog, yo, K2. 86 sts.

Row 42 (WS) Repeat row 28.

Repeat rows 29–42 until wrap reaches desired length minus approximately 7 inches (18cm) for remaining knot stitch, ending last repeat after a forty first row. The wrap in the photograph has 18 repeats of the crossed-eyelet-stitch pattern.

Change to knot stitch.

Row 280 (WS) Repeat row 28.

Row 281 (RS) Sl1P, K1, yo, K2tog, yo, K5, yo, K4, SM, * P1, K8, P1; repeat from * to next marker, SM, K4, yo, K5, yo, K2tog, yo, K2.

Rows 282–307 Repeat rows 2–27.

Row 308 Repeat row 4.

Bind off loosely on RS as follows:
Using Size 10 needles, * K2tog loosely, slip the stitch just made on RHN back to LHN; repeat from *.

FINISHING

Weave in ends.

Block by the damp-finishing method (see page 138).

"Leigh's Night Out" Bag   Leigh Radford

MATERIALS

Three 3½oz (100g) balls Leigh Radford/Lantern Moon Silk Gelato,
    shade Melon (Yarn A)

One 3½oz (100g) ball Leigh Radford/Lantern Moon Silk Gelato, shade
    Grape (Yarn B)

Three 1¾oz (50g) skeins Muench Yarns Touch Me, shade 3635 (Yarn C)

Pair Size 35 (20mm) knitting needles

Set of Size 19 (15mm) double-pointed needles or circular needle,
    16 inches (40cm) long

Purse frame, 10 inches (25cm) snap/spring frame

⅜ yard (35cm) of fabric for lining

Tapestry needle and sewing needle and thread

1 yard (1m) of contrasting ribbon, 2 inches (5cm) wide (optional)

One 3-inch (7.5cm) buckle (optional)

MEASUREMENTS

Width approximately 10 inches (25cm)

Length approximately 10 inches (25cm)

GAUGE

6 sts (one pattern repeat) = approximately 3–3½ inches (7.5–8cm)
and 8 rows (one pattern repeat) = approximately 2½ inches (6.5cm)
measured over two-tone lattice pattern on Size 35 needles or the
size required to obtain the correct gauge.

ABBREVIATIONS

See Page 129.

NOTES

Color A One strand of Silk Gelato (Melon) (Yarn A) and 2 strands
of Muench Yarns Touch Me (Yarn C) held together.

Color B One strand of Silk Gelato (Grape) (Yarn B).

BACK AND FRONT (Make 2)

Using Size 35 needles and Color A, cast on 28 sts.

Row 1 (WS) Knit.

Do not cut Color A.

Join Color B.

Row 2 (RS) Using Color B, K2, sl1wyib, * K4, sl2wyib; rep from *
to last 7 sts, K4, sl1wyib, K2.

Row 3 (WS) Using Color B, P2, sl1wyif, * P4, sl2wyif; rep from *
to last 7 sts, P4, sl1wyif, P2.

Row 4 Using Color A, K2, sl1wyib, * K4, sl2wyib; rep from * to last

7 sts, K4, sl1wyib, K2.

Row 5 Using Color A, K2, sl1wyif, * K4, sl2wyif; rep from * to last
7 sts, K4, sl1wyif, K2.

Row 6 Using Color B, K4, * sl2wyib, K4; rep from * to end.

Row 7 Using Color B, P4, * sl2wyif, P4; rep from * to end.

Row 8 Using Color A, K4, * sl2wyib, K4; rep from * to end.

Row 9 Using Color A, K4, * sl2wyif, K4; rep from * to end.

Repeat rows 2–9 once and then repeat rows 2–8.

Cut Color B.

Join Color A.

Work 4 rows in stockinette stitch beg with a purl row.

Bind off.

HANDLE

Using Size 19 double-pointed needles (or circular needle) and Color A,
cast on 3 sts.

Work an I-cord 21 inches (53cm) long (see pages 136–37).

Bind off, leaving a 5-inch (35cm) tail.

FINISHING

Join side and bottom seams with Yarn A or Yarn B.

Cut the lining fabric into a rectangle of 12 x 24 inches (30 x 61cm).
With right sides facing, fold in half lengthwise so the piece measures
12 x 12 inches (30 x 30cm). Beginning approximately 2 inches (5cm)
from the top, stitch ½-inch (1.5cm) seams on both sides. Fold top edge
of fabric over ¼ inch (5mm) and press. Slip lining through spring frame
and fold fabric over frame 1¾ inches (4.5cm) with wrong sides facing
each other. Sew facing to body of lining with blind (invisible) stitch on
WS. The fabric may be slightly wider than frame; if so, gather fabric
slightly around snap/spring frame. Insert completed lining into knitted
bag with WS of lining facing WS of bag and pin in place. Sew lining into
interior of knitted bag approximately ¼ inch (5mm) below the top edge.

Attach handle by threading tail from I-cord handle into tapestry needle
and thread through loop of purse frame. Pull I-cord through loop and
secure by threading tail through center of I-cord. Cut a 5-inch (13cm)
length of Yarn A or Yarn B and wrap at handle base as follows: Form a
loop where I-cord is threaded through metal loop of purse frame and
hold in place. Beginning approximately 1½–2 inches (4–5cm) up from loop,
wrap Yarn A or Yarn B around I-cord working back toward loop. Thread
the end through the loop and pull tight. Repeat for opposite end of handle.

Sew ribbon and buckle to outside of bag as shown.

made in Leigh's Silk Gelato yarn–Vietnamese silk cut into strips–this lush evening bag is perfect for a girlie "boho" look. Line it with crushed velvet or vintage fabric, and source a great buckle or brooch as the finishing touch.

What a great way to use the divine "Magic Balls" from Be Sweet yarns. With the simplest of patterns, you have a great shawl, wrap, throw, or scarf. The pattern is easy to adjust, depending on the size you prefer—you can make it longer or wider for a wrap or throw, narrower for a long skinny scarf, or shorter for a neck warmer. Or you can add more rows of the slubby yarn.

Sweetheart Shawl Nadine Curtis with Bardet Wardell

MATERIALS
One 1¾oz (50g) ball Be Sweet Slubby Mohair, shade Natural (Yarn A)
Two 1¾oz (50g) balls Be Sweet Magic Balls, shade Wild Berries (Yarn B)
Pair Size 15 (10mm) knitting needles

MEASUREMENTS
Length approximately 36 inches (92cm)
Width approximately 16½ inches (42cm)

GAUGE
9 sts and 16 rows (8 ridges) = 4 inches (10cm) square measured over garter stitch using Size 15 needles or the size required to obtain the correct gauge.

ABBREVIATIONS
See page 129.

NOTES
When using Yarn B, secure the knots when the ribbon ties are reached.

SHAWL
Using 10mm needles and Yarn A, cast on 38 sts loosely.
Row 1 (WS) Knit, leaving large loops.
Cut Yarn A.

Change to Yarn B.
Row 2 (RS) Knit.
Row 3 (WS) Knit.
Repeat rows 2 and 3 until both balls of Yarn B have been worked, ending with a WS row. If both balls of Yarn B look similar, reverse-wind the second ball so the shawl can be somewhat symmetrical.

Change to Yarn A.
Next row Knit loosely.

Bind off knitwise loosely, letting large loops remain.

FINISHING
Weave in ends.

VARIATION
The shawl can be made longer by using 3 balls of Yarn B and working the ends exactly the same.

this lace-stitch shawl in colors inspired by a "cameo" brooch is the height of divine knitting. The drape and the attention to detail will make you feel gorgeous as soon as you put it on. The flower corsage closure, replete with ribbons and buttons, makes it even more exquisite.

"Cameo" Shawl   Louisa Harding

MATERIALS

2(2, 3, 3) 1¾oz (50g) hanks Louisa Harding Sari Ribbon, shade 7 Shell (Yarn A)

2(3, 3, 4) 1¾oz (50g) balls Louisa Harding Glisten, shade 4, Gold (Yarn B)

4(4, 5, 5) 1¾oz (50g) balls Louisa Harding Grace, shade 2 Soft Gold (Yarn C)

Pair of Size 8 (5mm) knitting needles

Row counter

13 assorted mother-of-pearl buttons, approximately ⅜–¾ inch (1-2cm) diameter

MEASUREMENTS

To fit bust

30-32	34-36	38-40	42-44 inches
76-81	86-91	97-102	107-112cm

Shoulder width

33	35½	38	40¼ inches
84	90	96	102cm

Width (at widest)

38½	41¼	44	47 inches
98	105	112	119cm

Length (without hanging ribbons)

14	14	14	14 inches
35.5	35.5	35.5	35.5cm

GAUGE

18 sts and 28 rows = 4 inches (10cm) square measured over lace pattern using Size 8 needles or the size required to obtain the correct gauge.

ABBREVIATIONS

See page 129.

NOTES

When joining a new shade leave a tail of approximately 4 inches (10cm) for fringe around lower edge of wrap.

When short-row shaping, refer to the wrapping technique on page 133.

The number of stitches changes over the rows.

SHAWL

Using Size 8 needles and Yarn A, cast on 57 sts.

Work 2 rows in garter stitch.

Cut Yarn A.

Join Yarn B.

Work 2 rows in garter st.

Cut Yarn B.

Join Yarn C.

Work in lace and stripe pattern as follows:

Row 1 (RS) K10, K2tog, yo, K35, K2tog, yo, K8.

Row 2 K6, K2tog, yo, K2, P33, K2tog, yo, K2, P8, K2.

Row 3 K2, yo, [K2tog tbl, yo] twice, K4, K2tog, yo, K3, [yo, K2, K3tog, K2, yo, K1] 4 times, K2tog, yo, K8. 58 sts.

Row 4 K6, K2tog, yo, K2, P33, K2tog, yo, K2, P9, K2. 58 sts.

Row 5 K2, yo, K2, [K2tog tbl, yo] twice, K3, K2tog, yo, K3, [K1, yo, K1, K3tog, K1, yo, K2] 4 times, K2tog, yo, K8. 59 sts.

Row 6 K6, K2tog, yo, K2, P33, K2tog, yo, K2, P10, K2. 59 sts.

Row 7 K2, yo, K4, [K2tog tbl, yo] twice, K2, K2tog, yo, K3, [K2, yo, K3tog, yo, K3] 4 times, K2tog, yo, K8. 60 sts.

Row 8 K6, K2tog, yo, K2, P33, K2tog, yo, K2, P11, K2. 60 sts.

Row 9 K1, K2tog, yo, K2tog tbl, K1, [K2tog, yo] twice, K3, K2tog, yo, K3, [yo, K2, K3tog, K2, yo, K1] 4 times, K2tog, yo, K8. 59 sts.

Row 10 K6, K2tog, yo, K2, P33, K2tog, yo, K2, P10, K2. 59 sts.

Row 11 K1, K2tog, yo, K3tog, yo, K2tog, yo, K4, K2tog, yo, K3, [K1, K1, K3tog, K1, yo, K2] 4 times, K2tog, yo, K8. 58 sts.

Row 12 K6, K2tog, yo, K2, P33, K2tog, yo, K2, P9, K2. 58 sts.

Row 13 K1, K2tog, yo, K3tog, yo, K5, K2tog, yo, K3, [K2, yo, K3tog, yo, K3] 4 times, K2tog, yo, K8. 57 sts.

Row 14 K6, K2tog, yo, K2, P33, K2tog, yo, K2, P8, K2. 57 sts.

Cut Yarn C.

Join Yarn B.

Row 15 K10, K2tog, yo, K35, K2tog, yo, K8. 57 sts.

Row 16 K6, K2tog, yo, K35, K2tog, yo, K12. 57 sts.

Cut Yarn B.

Join Yarn A.

Row 17 K10, K2tog, yo, K35, K2tog, yo, K8. 57 sts.

Row 18 K6, K2tog, yo, K35, K2tog, yo, K12. 57 sts.

Cut Yarn A.

Join Yarn B.

Row 19 K10, K2tog, yo, K35, K2tog, yo, K8. 57 sts.

Row 20 K6, K2tog, yo, K35, K2tog, yo, K12. 57 sts.

Rows 1-20 form the lace and stripe pattern repeat.

Repeat rows 1-20 12(13, 14, 15) times then work rows 1-14 once.

Cut Yarn C.

Join Yarn B.

Work 2 rows garter st.

Cut Yarn B.

Join Yarn A.

Work 4 rows garter st.
Bind off using Yarn A.

FINISHING
Block the shawl following the instructions on page 138 and referring to the yarn labels.

Shoulder edging
With RS of shawl facing and starting at bind-off edge using Size 8 needles and Yarn A, pick up and knit 145(155, 165, 175) sts along straight edge of knitted piece.
Next row (WS) Knit.
Cut Yarn A.
Join Yarn B.
Row 1 (RS) * K1, sl1wyib; rep from * to last st, K1.
Row 2 * K1, yf, sl1wyif, yb; rep from * to last st, K1.
Join Yarn C.
Row 3 Knit.
Row 4 Knit.
Change to Yarn B.
Row 5 K1, * K1, sl1wyib; rep from * to last 2 sts, K2.
Row 6 K1, * K1, yf, sl1wyif, yb; rep from * to last 2 sts, K2.
Cut Yarn B.
Change to Yarn C.
Row 7 Knit.
Row 8 Knit.
Working in Yarn C only, repeat rows 1–8 once then rows 1–4 once.
Join Yarn B.
Row 21 K1, * K1, sl1wyib; rep from * to last 2 sts, K2.
Row 22 K1, * K1, yf, sl1wyif, yb; rep from * to last 2 sts, K2.
Change to Yarn C.
Row 23 Knit.
Row 24 Knit.
Cut Yarn C.
Change to Yarn B.
Row 25 * K1, sl1wyib; rep from * to last st, K1.
Row 26 * K1, yf, sl1wyif, yb; rep from * to last st, K1.
Cut Yarn B.
Join Yarn A.
Row 27 Knit.
Bind off knitwise on WS decreasing across row as follows:
Bind off 1, [K2tog, bind off, bind off 8], 14(15, 16, 17) times, bind off rem st.

Button edging
With RS of wrap facing and using Size 8 needles and Yarn A, pick up and knit 12 sts along left front edge of shoulder edging.
Bind off knitwise on WS.

Button loop edging
With RS of wrap facing and using Size 8 needles and Yarn A, pick up and knit 12 sts along right front edge of shoulder edging.
Next row (Button loop row) (WS) K1 (one stitch on RHN), * insert LHN from front to back into stitch on RHN and knit it; rep from * until a chain of 5 sts has been made. Then pick up first chain stitch made with LHN, knit this stitch again and then take last chain stitch made over this stitch (button loop made), cast off 3 sts (one stitch on RHN). Rep from * 3 times.
Sew buttons on left front to correspond with button loops.

Flower corsage
Two-color rosette (Make 2)
Using Size 8 needles and Yarn A, cast on 112 sts leaving a long tail.
Cut Yarn A, leaving a long tail.
Join Yarn C.
Row 1 Knit.
Row 2 K2, [K1, slip this st back onto LHN, lift the next 8 sts on LHN over this st and off needle, knit the first st again, K2] 10 times. 32 sts.
Row 3 Knit 24 sts, turn.
Row 4 Knit to end.
Row 5 Knit 16 sts, turn.
Row 6 Knit to end.
Row 7 Knit 8 sts, turn.
Row 8 Knit to end.
Cut yarn and thread through stitches on needle, pull tightly to create a rosette and secure with a few stitches. Do not sew in or trim Yarn A tails.

Small flowers (Make 7)
Using Size 8 needles and Yarn B, cast on 36 sts.
Row 1 * K1, bind off 4 sts (2 sts on needle); rep from * to end. 12 sts.
Cut yarn and thread yarn through sts on needle, pull tight and secure with a few stitches.

Arrange flowers on shoulder edging and sew in place using photograph as a guide.
Sew a button in the center of each flower.
Secure all lengths of yarn at lower edge of wrap and at the beginning and end of the first row of the rosettes to hang down like ribbons.
Cut all lengths of ribbons at a slanted angle to prevent them from fraying.

K nitted balls embellished with sparkling beads and the lush texture of the bouclé mohair in soft peach and gray makes this the prettiest and coziest neck warmer around.

Bouclé Neck Warmer   Juju Vail

MATERIALS

One 1¾oz (50g) ball Be Sweet Bouclé Mohair, shade Peach (Yarn A)

One 1¾oz (50g) ball Be Sweet Bouclé Mohair, shade Dark Gray (Yarn B)

One 1¾oz (50g) ball Louisa Harding Grace, shade 3 (Yarn C)

Pair each Size 8 (5mm) and 10½ (7mm) knitting needles

One Size 11 (8mm) knitting needle

16 crystal rose montee beads (or other 4mm crystals)

Fiberfill or other stuffing for knitted balls

Beading needle and thread

MEASUREMENTS

Length without cords and knitted balls 24½ inches (62cm)

Length with cords and knitted balls approximately 47 inches (120cm)

Width approximately 7 inches (18cm)

GAUGE

22 sts and 34 rows = 4 inches (10cm) square over stockinette stitch using Yarn C on Size 8 needles or the size required to obtain the correct gauge.

13 sts and 26 rows (13 ridges) = 4 inches (10cm) square over garter stitch using Yarn A on Size 10½ needles or the size required to obtain the correct gauge.

ABBREVIATIONS

See page 129.

FIRST KNITTED BALL

Using Size 8 needles and Yarn C, cast on 8 sts.

Row 1 (RS) Knit.

Row 2 Purl.

Row 3 (K1, M1) 8 times. 16 sts.

Row 4 Purl.

Row 5 * K1, M1, K2; rep from * to last st, K1, M1. 22 sts.

Work 7 rows st-st, beg and ending with a purl row.

Row 6 * K2tog, K2; rep from * to last 2 sts, K2tog. 16 sts.

Row 14 Purl.

Row 15 (K2tog) 8 times. 8 sts.

Row 16 Purl.

Row 17 Knit.

Row 18 (WS) Purl.

Do not bind off. Cut Yarn C.

FIRST CORD

Join Yarn B.

Row 1 (RS) K2tog, knit to end. 7 sts.

Row 2 P2tog, purl to end. 6 sts.

Cont in st-st until cord measures 10 inches (25cm), ending with a purl row.

Do not bind off. Cut Yarn B.

NECK WRAP

Change to Size 10½ needles and join Yarn A.

Row 1 (RS) (K1, M1) 6 times. 12 sts.

Row 2 Knit.

Row 3 (K1, M1, K2) 4 times. 16 sts.

Row 4 Knit.

Row 5 K2, (K1, M1, K3) 3 times, K1, M1, K1. 20 sts.

Row 6 Knit.

Cont in garter stitch without shaping until the neck wrap measures 24 inches (60cm) from the start of Yarn A, ending with a WS row.

Next row (RS) K2, (K2tog, K3) 3 times, K2tog, K1. 16 sts.

Next row Knit.

Next row (K2tog, K2) 4 times. 12 sts.

Next row Knit.

Next row (K2tog) 6 times. 6 sts.

Next row (WS) Knit.

Do not bind off. Cut Yarn A.

SECOND CORD

Change to 5mm needles and join Yarn B.

1st row (RS) Knit.

2nd row Purl.

Cont in st-st until cord measures 10 inches (25cm), ending with a purl row.

Next row (RS) K1, M1, knit to end. 7 sts.
2nd row P1, M1, purl to end. 8 sts.
Do not bind off. Cut Yarn B.

SECOND KNITTED BALL
Change to Size 8 needles and Yarn C.
Make the second knitted ball following
the instructions for the first knitted ball,
starting at row 1.
When complete, cut yarn leaving a long
tail. Thread the tail through all the stitches
on the needle and pull to close.

FINISHING
Block the wrap following the instructions on
page 138 and referring to the yarn labels.
Join bobble seam to within ½ inch (1cm) of top.
Add stuffing until the knitted ball is a nice round
shape then complete the seam.
Join cord seam using Yarn B to the beginning
of neck wrap section.
Repeat for the other bobble and cord.
Sew 8 crystal beads around the middle circumference
of each knitted ball.

RUFFLE
Using Size 10½ needles and Yarn B, with RS facing,
pick up and knits 70 stitches along one edge of neck
wrap section.
Row 1 (WS) Purl.
Row 2 (K1, M1) 70 times. 140 sts.
Row 3 Purl.
Bind off using a Size 11 needle.
Repeat ruffle on opposite edge.
Weave in ends of ruffle to meet the gray cord.

these pretty corsages are extremely versatile: Wear them on a lapel, hat, bag, or any other garment or accessory you wish to brighten up. Pile up two or three to create a bouquet of gorgeous knitted ruffles, or wear them singly. The patterns are straightforward and quick to make; it doesn't matter if they knit up smaller or larger than the pattern suggests, so any yarn can be used. In fact, scraps from your stash are an ideal place to start.

Flower Corsages   Claire Montgomerie

MATERIALS
One 1¾oz (50g) ball Debbie Bliss Alpaca Silk, shade 23 Bright
  Turquoise (Yarn A)
One 1¾oz (50g) ball Be Sweet Ribbon, shade Silver (Yarn B)
One 1¾oz (50g) ball ggh Bel Air, shade 21 Lime (Yarn C)
One 1¾oz (50g) ball Rowan Pure Wool DK, shade 042 Vivid Purple
  (Yarn D)
One 1¾oz (50g) ball Be Sweet Ribbon, shade Plum (Yarn F)
One 1¾oz (50g) ball Alchemy Synchronicity, shade Silver (Yarn F)
One 1¾oz (50g) ball Louisa Harding Fauve, shade 6 Lime (Yarn G)
One 1¾oz (50g) ball Rooster Almerino Aran, shade 303 Strawberry
  Cream (Yarn H)
One 1¾oz (50g) ball ggh Soft Kid, shade 55 Pale Pink (Yarn I)
Pair each Size 6 (4mm) and 10½ (6.5mm) knitting needles or the
  size appropriate for the yarn you decide to use
2 pairs Size 9 (5.5mm) knitting needles or the size appropriate for
  the yarn you decide to use
Large safety pins
Sewing needle and thread

MEASUREMENTS
Diameter at the widest point:
Corsage One 6½ inches (16cm)
Corsage Two 5½ inches (14cm)
Corsage Three 7 inches (18cm)

GAUGE
The correct gauge is not a requirement.

ABBREVIATIONS
See page 129.

Opposite: See page 92 for Cable Wrap pattern.

Fur st Fur stitch. Worked on RS rows. Knit the next stitch without letting it drop off LHN, bring the yarn forward between the needles, pass the yarn around your thumb or a piece of cardboard to make a loop approximately ¾ inches (2cm) long (or the desired length), take the yarn back between the needles, knit the stitch on the LHN again, this time completing it and letting it drop off the needle. Pass the first loop of the stitch just knitted (now on RHN) over the second loop of the stitch just knitted and off the needle to secure stitch.

CORSAGE ONE (CIRCULAR SHAPE)

First circle
Using Size 10½ needles and Yarn A, cast on 88 sts.
Cut Yarn A.
Join Yarn B.
Rows 1 and 2 Knit.
Row 3 * K9, K2tog; rep from * to end. 80 sts.
Row 4 Knit.
Row 5 * K8, K2tog; rep from * to end. 72 sts.
Row 6 Knit.
Row 7 * K7, K2tog; rep from * to end. 64 sts.
Row 8 Knit.
Row 9 * K6, K2tog; rep from * to end. 56 sts.
Row 10 Knit.
Row 11 * K5, K2tog; rep from * to end. 48 sts.
Row 12 Knit.
Row 13 * K4, K2tog; rep from * to end. 40 sts
Row 14 Knit.
Row 15 * K3, K2tog; rep from * to end. 32 sts.
Row 16 Knit.
Row 17 * K2, K2tog; rep from * to end. 24 sts.
Row 18 Knit.
Row 19 * K1, K2tog; rep from * to end. 16 sts.
Row 20 Knit.
Row 21 * K2tog; rep from * to end. 8 sts.
Cut yarn leaving approximately 12-inch (30cm) tail, thread through rem sts and pull up tight to draw into a circle. Join seam to complete circle.

Second circle
Using Size 10½ needles and Yarn C, cast on 80 sts.
Rows 1 and 2 Knit.
Work as for first circle from row 5 onward.

Opposite: You can use as many layers as you wish: The small corsage (top) is made up of the fourth and fifth circles of Corsage One, shown in its entirety below.

Third circle

Using Size 10½ needles and Yarn D, cast on 72 sts.
Cut Yarn D.
Join Yarn E.
Row 1 Knit.
Work as for first circle from row 7 onward.

Fourth circle

Using Size 6 needles and Yarn F, cast on 64 sts.
Row 1 Knit.
Row 2 Purl.
Work as for first circle from row 9 onward, but working even rows as purl instead of knit, thus working in stockinette stitch. When joining the seam, allow the cast-on edge to roll to the RS, as is natural with st-st.

Fifth circle

Using Size 10½ needles and Yarn G, cast on 30 sts.
Row 1 Knit.
Row 2 K1, * fur st 1; rep from * to last st, K1.
Row 3 Knit.
Cut yarn leaving approximately 12-inch (30cm) tail. Thread yarn through rem stitches and pull, making strip curl in on itself. Sew in place in center of fourth circle as a curled rosette.

FINISHING

Layer the circles on top of one another, largest at the bottom to smallest at the top, and sew in place.
Make as many layers as desired, leaving out or adding in layers as you wish.

Attach the brooch back or pin to the back of the corsage, toward the top center to prevent the layers from drooping.

CORSAGE TWO (FLOWER SHAPE)

First layer—strip one

Using Size 10½ needles and Yarn E, cast on 90 sts.
Row 1 Purl.
Row 2 K2, * K1 and slip this st back onto LHN, with the tip of RHN, lift next 8 sts after the first st, one at a time, over and off LHN, yo2, knit first st on LHN again, K2; rep from * to end.
Row 3 Knit, drop first yo of previous row, work [K1, K1 tbl, K1] into second yo. 50 sts.
Place all stitches on a holder.

First layer—strip two

Using Size 10½ needles and Yarn H, cast on 106 sts.
Rows 1 and 2 Purl.
Row 3 K2, * K1 and slip this st back onto LHN, with the tip of RHN, lift next 10 sts after the first st, one at a time, over and off LHN, yo2, knit first st on LHN again, K2; rep from * to end.
Row 4 K1 * P2tog, drop first yo of previous row, [K1, P1, K1, P1] into second yo, P1; rep from * to last st, K1. 50 sts.
Row 5 Knit.
Place all sts on a holder.

First layer—strip three

Using Size 10½ needles and Yarn F, cast on 114 sts.
Rows 1-3 Purl.
Row 4 K2, * K1 and slip this st back onto LHN, with the tip of RHN, lift next 11 sts after the first st, one at a time, over and off LHN, yo2, knit the first st on LHN again, K2; rep from * to end.
Row 5 K1 * P2tog, drop first yo of previous row, [K1, P1, K1, P1] into second yo, P1; rep from * to last st, K1. 50sts.
Row 6 Knit.
Row 7 Knit, while at the same time joining the second strip of petals. Hold the needle containing the stitches from Strip Three and the stitch holder containing the stitches from Strip Two together in your left hand. WS of Strip Two should be against RS of Strip Three. Insert RHN knitwise into the first stitch on the front needle and then insert the tip of RHN into the first stitch on the back needle and knit these two stitches together onto RHN.
Row 8 Knit.
Row 9 Knit, while at the same time joining the first strip of petals as described in row 7.
Row 10 * K2tog, K3; rep from * to end. 40 sts.

Attach the brooch back or pin to the back of the corsage, toward the top center to prevent the layers from drooping.

CORSAGE THREE (PETAL SHAPE)

First layer—strip one

Using Size 9 needles and Yarn F, cast on 5 sts.

Row 1 (WS) P1, M1, purl to last st, M1, P1. 7 sts.

Row 2 K1, M1, knit to last st, M1, K1. 9 sts.

Rows 3, 5, and 7 Purl.

Row 4 K1, M1, knit to last st, M1, K1. 11 sts.

Row 6 K1, M1, knit to last st, M1, K1. 13 sts.

Row 8 K1, M1, knit to last st, M1, K1. 15 sts.

Work 5 rows st-st, beg and ending with a purl row.

Row 14 K5, skpo, K1, K2tog, K5. 13 sts.

Rows 15, 17, 19, and 21 Purl.

Row 16 K4, skpo, K1, K2tog, K4. 11 sts.

Row 18 K3, skpo, K1, K2tog, K3. 9 sts.

Row 20 K2, skpo, K2tog, K2. 7 sts.

Row 22 K1, skpo, K1, K2tog, K1. 5 sts.

Row 23 Purl.

Leave this petal on the needle. Make 5 more, leaving each on the needle next to the last. Alternatively, the petals can be left on a stitch holder.

First layer—strip two

Using Size 9 needles and Yarn C, cast on 5 sts.

Row 1 (WS) Purl.

Row 2 K1, M1, knit to last st, M1, K1. 7 sts.

Rows 3 and 5 Purl.

Row 4 K1, M1, knit to last st, M1, K1. 9 sts.

Row 6 K1, M1, knit to last st, M1, K1. 11 sts.

Work 5 rows st-st, beg and ending with a purl row.

Row 12 K3, skpo, K1, K2tog, K3. 9 sts.

Rows 13 and 15 Purl.

Row 14 K2, skpo, K1, K2tog, K2. 7 sts.

Row 16 K1, skpo, K1, K2tog, K1. 5 sts.

Row 17 Purl.

Leave this petal on the needle. Make 7 more, leaving each on the needle next to the last. Alternatively, the petals can be left on a stitch holder.

First layer—strip three

Using Size 9 needles and Yarn H, cast on 3 sts.

Rows 1, 3, and 5 (WS) Purl.

Row 2 K1, M1, knit to last st, M1, K1. 5 sts.

Row 4 K1, M1, knit to last st, M1, K1. 7 sts.

Above: Flower-shaped Corsage Two.

Right: The centers of the corsages can be worn on their own, without the surrounding petals, as shown on page 70. This is the center of Corsage Three.

Row 11 Knit.

Row 12 * K2tog, K2; rep from * to end. 30 sts.

Row 13 Knit.

Row 14 * K2tog, K1; rep from * to end. 20 sts.

Row 15 Knit.

Row 16 *K2tog; rep from * to end. 10 sts.

Cut yarn leaving approximately 12-inch (30cm) tail, thread through rem sts and pull up tight to draw into a circle. Join seam to complete circle.

Second layer

Using Size 10½ needles and holding Yarns D, F, G, and I together, cast on 3 sts.

Work 4 inches (10cm) garter stitch.

Bind off first stitch and fasten off second stitch. Let the last stitch unravel back down to cast-on edge.

Roll up the strip into a circle, with loops on top, and sew in place.

FINISHING

Lay the second layer on top of the first, in the center of the petals, and sew in place.

Row 6 K1, M1, knit to last st, M1, K1. 9 sts.

Work 5 rows st-st, beg and ending with a purl row.

Row 12 K2, skpo, K1, K2tog, K2. 7 sts.

Row 13 Purl.

Row 14 K1, skpo, K1, K2tog, K1. 5 sts.

Row 15 Purl.

Leave this petal on the needle. Make 7 more, leaving each on the needle next to the last. Alternatively, the petals can be left on a stitch holder. Do not cut Yarn H.

Assemble all petals in order, with RS facing for the next row, with the first petal made at the knob end of LHN and the last petal made at the tip of LHN.

Continuing in Yarn H, knit first 4 stitches of last petal made, knit together last stitch of petal and first stitch of next. Continue in this way, knitting together the last and first stitches of each petal until the last six, largest petals, are reached. Knit along these, joining them, yet not knitting together the stitches of adjoining petals, but just knitting along the 5 stitches of each petal normally. 95 sts.

Work 4 rows garter stitch on these 95 sts.

Bind off knitwise.

Second layer

Using Size 10½ needles and Yarn B, cast on 64 sts.

Rows 1-3 Knit.

Work as for first circle of Corsage One from row 9, and sew up accordingly.

Third layer

Using Size 10½ needles and Yarn I, cast on 4 sts.

Work in garter stitch for approximately 8 inches (20cm).

Bind off first st and fasten off second stitch. Let the last 2 stitches unravel back down to cast-on edge.

Fourth layer

Using Size 10½ needles and Yarns A, G, and I held together, cast on 20 sts.

Row 1 K1, * fur st 1; rep from * to last st, K1.

Cut yarn leaving approximately 12-inch (30cm) tail, thread yarn through rem sts and pull up, making strip roll into a rosette. Secure in place.

FINISHING

Lay out the first layer in a rosette, with largest leaves on the bottom, spiraling up to the small pink petals, and sew in place. If the yarn used is fairly soft, the leaves may need to be secured with a few stitches so they don't flop down when worn.

Lay the second layer on top and sew in place.

Lay the last two layers in the center of the second layer, with the third layer wrapped around the fourth layer, and secure.

Attach the pin to the back of the corsage, toward the top center to prevent the layers from drooping.

Right: Petal-shaped Corsage Three.

No girl can have too many bags, and this pretty blue one is ideal for knitting, shopping, or work. The rows of bobbly raspberry stitch and threaded ribbon elevate the simple rectangular shape into the loveliest bag. Line it with lovely fabric and finish with great Lucite, wood, or bamboo handles.

Raspberry-Stitch Bag Kate Samphier

MATERIALS
Eight 1¾oz (50g) balls Frog Tree Chunky Alpaca, shade 61
Pair Size 8 (5mm) knitting needles
Pair bag handles (these have a straight opening 11½ inches/29cm wide)
18 inches (50cm) of lining fabric; matching sewing thread and needle
Two 1-yard (1m) lengths of cream ribbon, 1¼ inches (3cm) wide
Two 20-inch (50cm) lengths of cream ribbon, 1¼ inches (3cm) wide

MEASUREMENTS
Width approximately 15½ inches (39cm)
Length without handles approximately 14 inches (35cm)

GAUGE
20 stitches and 24 rows = 4 inches (10cm) square measured over stockinette stitch using Size 8 needles or the size required to obtain the correct gauge.

ABBREVIATIONS
See page 129.

BAG
Using Size 8 needles, cast on 83 sts.
Work 12 rows in stockinette stitch, beginning with a knit row.

Ribbon eyelet panel
** **Row 1 (RS)** Knit.
Rows 2 and 4 Knit.
Row 3 * K2tog tbl, yo; rep from * to last st, K1.

Stockinette-stitch panel
Work 8 rows st-st, inc 1 st at end of last row. 84 sts.

Raspberry-stitch panel
Row 1 (RS) Purl.
Row 2 * (K1, P1, K1) into next stitch, P3tog; rep from * to end.
Row 3 Purl.

Row 4 * P3tog, (K1, P1, K1) into next stitch; rep from * to end.
Repeat rows 1-4 four times.
Next row (RS) Purl, dec 1 st at end of row. 83 sts.

Stockinette-stitch panel
Beg and ending with a purl (WS) row, work 7 rows st-st. **
Rep from ** to ** 4 times.

Ribbon eyelet panel
Row 1 (RS) Knit.
Rows 2 and 4 Knit.
Row 3 * K2tog tbl, yo; rep from * to last st, K1.
Beg with a knit row, work 12 rows st-st.
Bind off.

FINISHING
Block following instructions on page 138 and referring to the yarn label.
Cut lining fabric to size of knitted piece plus a seam allowance of ½ inch (1.5cm) all round. PM at each side edge of knitted piece halfway along first raspberry-stitch panel from cast-on edge. Repeat for bound-off edge. PM at corresponding points on lining fabric.
Fold knitting in half, WS facing, so cast-on edge meets bound off edge and central eyelet panel is at fold. Join side seams between bottom of bag and markers.
Thread 20-inch (50cm) lengths of ribbon through the eyelets closest to cast-on and bound-off edges and secure ends.
Fold lining in half widthwise and join side seams to the markers. Fold over the unsewn length of side edge to WS of lining and press.
With WS of lining facing WS of bag, insert lining into bag.
Insert cast-on edge of bag through one handle, from RS to WS, and fold over stockinette stitch on WS, with ribbon eyelet panel remaining on RS. Stitch cast-on edge in place. Repeat for bound-off edge.
Fold over top of lining to WS and sew in place to cover cast-on and bound-off edges. Sew lining in place at side edges.
Thread a 1-yard (1m) length of ribbon through the eyelets across the center of each side of the bag. Knot ends of ribbon together.

ell-shaped flowers dangle on their stems from the seed-stitch bow of this quirky brooch. For variation, add beads in the centers or alternate flowers with baby pompoms. You could also make a cluster of flowers and hang them on a crocheted string to make a necklace.

Bell-Flower Brooch   Julie Arkell

MATERIALS

One 1¾oz (50g) ball ggh Bel Air in each of five shades: 1 Light Pink,
   3 Deep Plum, 5 Bright Pink, 9 Burnt Orange and 21 Mustard for the
   flowers, bobbles, and bows (Yarn A)
One 1¾oz (50g) ball ggh Bel Air, shade 19 Green for the stems (Yarn B)
Pair Size 3 (3.25mm) knitting needles
Two Size 3 (3.25mm) double-pointed knitting needles
Tapestry needle
Large safety pin

MEASUREMENTS

Brooch approximately 4 x 6 inches (10 x 15cm)
Bell flower (without knitted ball) approximately 2 inches (5cm)

GAUGE

The correct gauge is not a requirement.

ABBREVIATIONS

See page 129.

NOTE

The flowers, knitted balls, and bows are made in assorted colors of
the knitter's choice (Yarn A).

BELL FLOWER (Make 5 in different colors)

Using Size 3 needles and Yarn A, cast on 15 sts.
Beg with a knit row, work 8 rows in stockinette stitch.
Row 9 * K3, K2tog; rep from * to end. 12 sts.
Rows 10, 12, and 14 Purl.
Row 11 * K2, K2tog; rep from * to end. 9 sts.
Row 13 * K2, K2tog; rep from * once, K1. 7 sts.
Row 15 * K1, K2tog; rep from * once, K1. 5 sts.
Row 16 Purl.
Cut yarn leaving a tail approximately 8 inches (20cm) long. Thread
tail through remaining stitches, gather the stitches and leave.

STEM (Make 5)

Using Size 3 double-pointed needles and Yarn B, cast on 3 sts.
Work an I-cord 4 inches (10cm) long (see page 136-37).
Bind off.

BOBBLES (Make 5 in different colors)

Using Size 3 needles and Yarn A, cast on 1 stitch, leaving a long tail.

Row 1 (WS) [K1 into the front and K1 into the back of the stitch]
3 times. 6 sts.
Rows 2 and 4 (RS) Purl.
Rows 3 and 5 Knit.
Row 6 [P2tog] 3 times. 3 sts.
Row 7 Sl1, K2tog, psso. 1 st.
Fasten off, leaving a long tail.
To form the knitted ball, thread one of the tails through a tapestry
needle and work a running stitch around the shape. Pull the thread
firmly to form a knitted ball, leaving the other tail hanging free–this
will go through the bell flower.

BOW

Using Size 3 needles and Yarn A, cast on 7 sts.
1st row K1, * P1, K1; rep from * to end.
Repeating row 1 forms seed stitch.
Work 27 more rows in seed st.
Bind off in seed stitch.

BOW CENTER

Using Size 3 needles and Yarn A, cast on 5 sts.
Work 12 rows in seed st as for the bow.
Bind off in seed stitch.

FINISHING

Find middle of bow and work running stitch up the center,
gathering slightly.
Take center piece of bow and stitch the top edge onto back of bow,
about ¼ inch (5mm) from bow edge. Repeat at the bottom.
Thread the tapestry needle with the tail at the top of a bell flower.
Choose a contrasting knitted ball to hang down the center, making
sure it can be seen below bottom opening of flower.
Pass the long tail of the knitted ball through the top of the flower and
then pull the top of the flower tight to secure. Then sew a seam at
the back of the flower to form bell shape.
Turn up cast-on edge a little so the reverse stockinette stitch of bell
flower can be seen.
Sew in bound-off tails on stems. With the cast-on tail sew a stem to
a bell flower.
When all five flowers are completed gather them together, with
seams at the back, so they hang unevenly.
Sew stems to the back of bow.
Sew a large safety pin onto back of bow.

this pattern can be adapted in many different ways. In addition to this version, a necklace may be composed of many small bows strung together, just one large one, or any combination of sizes you wish; it is also possible to attach a single bow to a pin to wear as a brooch. The bows can be knitted in any yarn, using up odd balls from a stash. This silk has been chosen for its weight, drape, and sheen, making the bows hang as prettily as jewels.

Bow Necklace Claire Montgomerie

MATERIALS
One 1¾oz (50g) ball Debbie Bliss Pure Silk, shade 009 Lilac (Yarn A)
One 1¾oz (50g) ball Debbie Bliss Pure Silk, shade 003 Cream (Yarn B)
Pair Size 6 (4mm) knitting needles or size appropriate for the yarn used
One Size 000 (3mm) crochet hook
Button to fasten, approximately ¼-⅜ inch (6-8mm) diameter

MEASUREMENTS
Length from top of bow to end of tie
Large bow approximately 8 inches (20cm)
Small bow approximately 3¼ inches (8cm)

GAUGE
The correct gauge is not a requirement.

LARGE BOW
Using Size 6 needles and Yarn A, cast on 9 sts.
Row 1 K1, * P1, K1; rep from * to end.
Repeating row 1 forms seed stitch.
Cont in seed stitch until strip measures 24½ inches (62cm).
Bind off in seed stitch.

Bow center
Using Size 6 needles and Yarn B, cast on 7 sts.
Work in seed stitch as for the bow until strip measures 2½ inches (6cm).
Bind off in seed stitch.

Fold the long strip into a bow shape, crossing the ends over at the back. Fasten by wrapping the short strip around the middle where the bow folds over itself. Sew the ends of the short strip together at the back to finish and secure with a few stitches through the bow center if desired.

SMALL BOW (Make 2)
Using Size 6 needles and Yarn B, cast on 5 sts.
Work in seed stitch as for the large bow until strip measures 12 inches (30cm).
Bind off in seed stitch.

Bow center
Using Size 6 needles and Yarn B, cast on 5 sts.
Work in seed stitch as for the large bow until strip measures 1½ inches (4cm).
Bind off in seed stitch.

Make the small bow as for the large bow.

NECKLACE
Using a Size 000 crochet hook and Yarn B, make a length of chain 6 inches (15cm) long or desired length. Make a second chain 1¼ inches (3cm) longer than the first, then make a loop at the end by working 1 slip st into the chain 1¼ inches (3cm) from hook.
Sew the button onto one end of the shorter chain and use the loop on the second chain as a buttonhole to fasten.

FINISHING
Sew one small bow to each side of the large bow, joining the folded parts. Sew one chain to each small bow at the center back. Weave in all ends.

beautiful boudoirs

avender is renowned for its soothing, sleep-inducing properties, and this sweet lavender-filled pillow makes a cozy decoration for a bed while giving off a calming and relaxing aroma. The dusky pink wool cover is knitted in a mixture of diamond pattern and bird cable stripe, creating a textural design that is offset by the luxe velvet ribbon.

Lavender Sleep Pillow   **Ruth Cross**

MATERIALS
Five 1¾oz (50g) balls Rowan Little Big Wool, shade 504 Amethyst
Pair Size 10½ (7mm) knitting needles
1 square yard (1 square meter) of matching cotton fabric
Several scoops of dried lavender
½ yard (50cm) matching double-sided velvet ribbon, ¾ inch (2cm) wide
Sewing needle and thread

MEASUREMENTS
Width of main piece before folding 26¾ inches (68cm)
Width after folding 16½ inches (42cm)
Height, top to bottom 12½ inches (32cm)

GAUGE
13 sts and 18 rows = 4 inches (10cm) square measured over stockinette stitch on Size 10½ needles or the size required to obtain the correct gauge.
If your gauge is correct for stockinette stitch, it will be correct for the pattern.

ABBREVIATIONS
See page 129.
Cable 6 Slip next 2 stitches onto a cable needle and hold at back of work, K1 from LHN, K2 from cable needle, then slip next stitch onto a cable needle and hold at front of work, K2 from LHN, K1 from cable needle.

NOTES
Refer to the special cast-on, knit, and purl techniques described on pages 31–32.

Making a buttonhole
Bring yarn to front of work, slip 1 stitch from LHN to RHN, pass yarn between the needles to back of work and leave.

Slip another stitch from LHN to RHN, pass the first stitch over it—
1 stitch bound off. Repeat this process until 4 stitches for buttonhole
have been bound off.

Slip the loop on RHN back to LHN and turn work.

Pick up hanging yarn and pass it between the needles to back of
work. Now cast on 5 stitches using the cable cast-on (see page 130).
Before placing last loop on LHN, bring yarn through the needles to
the front forming a dividing strand between the last stitch and the
next-to-last stitch. Turn work again.

Slip the first stitch from LHN to RHN, then pass the last (extra) cast-
on stitch over it. Buttonhole completed. Continue working across row.

PILLOW COVER

Using Size 10½ needles, cast on 111 stitches.

Row 1 (WS) Purl.

Row 2 (RS) K2, sl2wyib, K2, [K1, yo, K3, K2tog, K4, yo] 3 times, K1, yo,
K3, K2tog, K2, sl2wyib, K5, yo, K3, K2tog, K4, yo, K5, sl2wyib, K7, yo,
[K1, yo, K3 K2tog, K4, yo] 3 times, K3, sl2wyib, K2. 119 sts.

Row 3 P2, sl2wyif, P2, [P5, P2tog, P4] 3 times, P5, P2tog, P2, sl2wyif,
P9, P2tog, P9, sl2wyif, P7, [P5, P2tog, P4] 3 times, P3, sl2wyif, P2.
111 sts.

Row 4 Cable 6, [K2, yo, K2, K2tog, K3, yo, K1] 3 times, K2, yo, K2,
K2tog, cable 6, K4, yo, K2, K2tog, K3, yo, K4, cable 6, K4, yo, K1, [K2,
yo, K2, K2tog, K3, yo, K1] 3 times, K1, cable 6. 119 sts.

Row 5 P6, [P5, P2tog, P4] 3 times, P5, P2tog, P13, P2tog, P18, [P5,
P2tog, P4] 3 times, P7 111 sts

Row 6 K2, sl2wyib, K2, [K3, yo, K1, K2tog, K2, yo, K2] 3 times, K3, yo,
K1, K2tog, K2, sl2wyib, K7, yo, K1, K2tog, K2, yo, K7, sl2wyib, K5, yo, K3,
[K2, yo, K1, K2tog, K2, yo, K3] 3 times, K2, sl2wyib, K2. 119 sts.

Row 7 P2, sl2wyif, P2, [P5, P2tog, P4] 3 times, P5, P2tog, P2, sl2wyif,
P9, P2tog, P9, sl2wyif, P2, P5, [P5, P2tog, P4] 3 times, P3, sl2wyif, P2.
111 sts.

Row 8 Cable 6, [K4, yo, K2tog, K1, yo, K3] 3 times, K4, yo, K2tog, cable
6, K6, yo, K2tog, K1, yo, K6, cable 6, K2, yo, K4, [K3, yo, K2tog, K1, yo,
K4] 3 times, cable 6. 119 sts.

Row 9 Repeat row 5. 111 sts.

Row 10 K2, sl2wyib, K7, [yo, K1, yo, K3, K2tog, K4] 3 times, yo, K3,
sl2wyib, K2, yo, K1, K2tog, K4, yo, K1, yo, K3, K2tog, K2, yo, K2, sl2wyib,
K3, yo, [K3, K2tog, K4, yo, K1, yo] 3 times, K3, K2tog, K2, sl2wyib, K2.
120 sts.

Row 11 P2, sl2wyif, P12, [P2tog, P9] twice, P2tog, P7, sl2wyif, P4, P2tog,
P9, P2tog, P4, sl2wyif, P7, [P2tog, P9] 3 times, P2tog, P2, sl2wyif, P2.
111 sts.

Row 12 Cable 6, K4, [yo, K3, yo, K2, K2tog, K3] 3 times, yo, K2,
cable 6, yo, K1, K2tog, K3, yo, K3, yo, K2, K2tog, K2, yo, cable 6, K2,
[yo, K2, K2tog, K3, yo, K3] 3 times, yo, K2, K2tog, cable 6. 120 sts.

Row 13 P16, [P2tog, P9] twice, P2tog, P13, P2tog, P9, P2tog, P13,
[P2tog, P9] 3 times, P2tog, P6. 111 sts.

Row 14 K2, sl2wyib, K5, [yo, K5, yo, K1, K2tog, K2] 3 times, yo, K5,
sl2wyib, K2, yo, K1, K2tog, K2, yo, K5, yo, K1, K2tog, K2, yo, K2, sl2wyib,
K5, [yo, K1, K2tog, K2, yo, K5] 3 times, yo, K1, K2tog, K2, sl2wyib, K2.
120 sts.

Row 15 Repeat row 11. 111 sts.

Row 16 Cable 6, K2, [yo, K7, yo, K2tog, K1] 3 times, yo, K4, cable 6, K1,
yo, K2tog, K1, yo, K7, yo, K2tog, K1, yo, K1, cable 6, K4, [yo, K2tog, K1,
yo, K7] 3 times, yo, K2tog, cable 6. 120 sts.

Row 17 Repeat row 13. 111 sts.

Rows 2–17 form the pattern.

Repeat rows 2–12 once.

Next row P2, make buttonhole, P10, [P2tog, P9] twice, P2tog, P13,
P2tog, P9, P2tog, P13, [P2tog, P9] 3 times, P2tog, make buttonhole, P2.

Repeat rows 14–17 once.

Repeat rows 2–17 once more.

Repeat rows 2–11 once.

58 rows pattern worked in all.

Bind off knitwise.

PILLOW UNDERFLAP

Using Size 10½ needles, cast on 30 sts.

Row 1 (RS) Knit.

Row 2 Purl.

Repeating these 2 rows forms stockinette stitch.

Cont in st-st until the underflap measures the same length as
the body, ending with a purl row.

Bind off knitwise.

FINISHING

Fold the short sides of the cover toward the center, right sides together,
so the cables on the front and back match. Pin these ends in place.
Then center the underflap over the gap so the knit side is showing
(the purl side will show on the outside when it's finished).
Sew along the top and bottom and turn right side out.

To make the lavender pillow

Measure the folded knitted pillow cover and cut 2 pieces of matching
fabric to the same size, adding a ¾-in (2cm) seam allowance to the
length and width.
Sew ¼ inch (1cm) in from the edge nearly all the way around and
turn right side out.
Fill with lavender through the gap and neatly sew up the opening.
Insert the pillow into the knitted cover and use the ribbon to draw
the two sides together.

Floral Bolster Pillow   Catherine Tough

MATERIALS

Three 3½oz (100g) balls Rowan Big Wool, shade 37 Zing (Yarn A)
One 1¾oz (50g) ball ggh Bel Air, shade 01 Light Pink (Yarn B)
One 1¾oz (50g) ball ggh Bel Air, shade 20 Olive Green (Yarn C)
One 1¾oz (50g) ball ggh Bel Air, shade 11 Brown (Yarn D)
One 1¾oz (50g) ball ggh Bel Air, shade 03 Red (Yarn E)
One 1¾oz (50g) ball ggh Bel Air, shade 19 Green (Yarn F)
Pair each Size 8 (5mm) and 19 (12mm) knitting needles
Pillow form to fit (approximately 22 x 22 inches/55 x 55cm folded in half)
Invisible monofilament thread or matching sewing thread and needle
Wooden button, approximately 1½ inches (3.5cm) diameter

MEASUREMENTS

12 x 21½ inches (30 x 55cm)

GAUGE

7½ sts and 10 rows = 4 inches (10cm) square measured over stockinette stitch using Big Wool and Size 19 needles or the size required to obtain the correct gauge.
16 sts and 22 rows = 4 inches (10cm) square measured over stockinette stitch before felting using Bel Air and Size 8 needles or the size required to obtain the correct gauge.

ABBREVIATIONS

See page 129.

NOTE

The main part of this bolster is basically a rectangle and is knit in seven alternating sections of garter and stockinette stitch.

BOLSTER COVER

Using Size 19 needles and Big Wool, cast on 25 stitches.
Work in garter st until bolster cover measures 7 inches (18cm).
Beg with a knit row, work in st-st for 4¼ inches (11cm) (until bolster cover measures 11¼ inches/29cm), ending with a RS (knit) row.
Work in garter st for 8¾ inches (22cm) (until bolster cover measures 20 inches (51cm), ending with a WS row.
Work in st-st for 10½ inches (27cm) (until bolster cover measures 30½ inches/78cm), ending with a RS row.
Work in garter st for 6 inches (15cm) (until bolster cover measures 36½ inches/93cm), ending with a WS row.
Work in st-st for 8 inches (20cm) (until bolster cover measures 44½ inches/113cm), ending with a RS row.

Work in garter st for 1¼ inches (3cm) (until bolster cover measures 45¾ inches/116cm), ending with a WS row.
Work in st-st for ¾ inch (2cm) (until bolster cover measures 46½ inch/118cm), ending with a WS row.

Bind-off and buttonhole row (RS) Bind off 12 stitches then * wind the yarn around the RHN and bring it through the loop on the RHN. Repeat from * 4 times. Knit together the next two stitches on the LHN and bind off the next stitch on the RHN to make a neat finish on the button loop. Complete the bind-off to the end of the row.

PM at both ends of the center row (23¼ inches/59cm from each short edge).

FLOWERS (Make 2, one in Yarn B and one in Yarn C)
Using Size 8 needles and Yarn B, cast on 32 sts.
Beg with a knit row, work 8 inches (20cm) st-st.
Bind off.
The piece will measure approx 8 x 8 inches (20 x 20cm).

Felting

The pieces are felted until they are stable enough to be cut and not fray. This can be done by hand, alternately washing in hot and cold water while rubbing with liquid detergent. Alternatively, use your washing machine. It's best to start with the "warm" setting, then more up to "hot" if necessary to obtain the desired result. Felting will shrink the knitted pieces.

FINISHING

Block each piece following the instructions on page 138 and referring to the yarn labels, or gently press using a steam iron and leave until dry.
Fold the buttonhole edge of the cover to the center row. Fold the other short edge beyond the center row to form an underlap on the RS until the finished cover measures 21½ inches (55cm) long. Pin in place and join the side seams.
Cut out petals and leaves from the felted pieces and place them on the cover. They can be attached temporarily with double-sided tape or pins until you are happy with the design.
Hand-stitch round the petals using an invisible or matching thread. Embroider the stems in backstitch and embroider buds and highlights using Yarns D, E, and F.
Sew on the button.
Insert the pillow form into the cover.

perfect on a bed, sofa, armchair, or daybed, this lovely bolster pillow is knitted in garter stitch and stockinette stitch, creating a gorgeous textured effect. There are charming clusters of flowers, twigs, and felted leaves in contrasting colors, of which you can make more or fewer depending on the look you are after.

Melt back into your comfort zone. Like the Danish word "hygge," which means cozy, warm, and glowing—this luxurious hot-water bottle cover makes you feel happy. With its chunky cream yarn knitted into rows of pretty cables and the velvet ribbon tie, it looks gorgeous on the bed any time of day and is an irresistible bedfellow on cold nights.

Hot-Water Bottle Cover

Ruth Cross

MATERIALS
Four 3½oz (100g) balls Blue Sky Alpacas Bulky, shade 1004 Polar
Pair Size 10½ (7mm) knitting needles
Cable needle
Row counter
1½ yards (1.5m) pale pink double-sided velvet ribbon, ¾ inch (2cm) wide

MEASUREMENTS
Cover width 9⅝ inches (24.5cm)
Length to ribbon holes 11½ inches (29cm)
Length above ribbon holes 3¼ inches (8cm)
Cast-on edge width 19¼ inches (49cm)
Length one cable repeat 1½ inches (4cm)

GAUGE
11½ sts and 13½ rows = 4 inches (10cm) square over stitch pattern using Blue Sky Alpacas Bulky and Size 10½ needles or the size required to obtain the correct gauge.

ABBREVIATIONS
See page 129.
C4B Slip next 2 sts onto cable needle and hold at back of work, K2 from LHN then K2 from cable needle.
C4F Slip next 2 sts onto cable needle and hold at front of work, K2 from LHN then K2 from cable needle.

HOT-WATER BOTTLE COVER
Using Size 10½ needles, cast on 57 sts.
Row 1 (RS) Knit.
Rows 2, 4, and 6 P21, [yo, sl1wyif, P2tog, psso, yo, P2] twice, P1, [yo, sl1wyif, P2tog, psso, yo, P2] 5 times.
Rows 3 and 5 K48, yo, sl1wyib, K2tog, psso, yo, K2, yo, sl1wyib, K2tog, psso, yo, K1.
Row 7 K38, C4B, C4F, K2, yo, sl1wyib, K2tog, psso, yo, K2, yo, sl1wyib, K2tog, psso, yo, K1.
Repeat rows 2-7 five times, then repeat rows 2 and 3 once.

Row 40 (WS) P16, [yo, sl1wyif, P2tog, psso, yo, P2] 3 times, P1, [yo, sl1wyif, P2tog, psso, yo, P2] 5 times. PM at both ends of this row.
Row 41 K43, [yo, sl1wyib, K2tog, psso, yo, K2] twice, yo, sl1wyib, K2tog, psso, yo, K1.
Repeat rows 40 and 41 four times.
Bind off knitwise on WS.

FINISHING
Block the cover following the instructions on page 138 and referring to the yarn label.
Fold the cover in half and join the side and bottom seams.
On row 40, use the natural holes on either side of each twist stripe where the cable ends to thread the ribbon.

This page: See page 30 for 'Isobel' Gilet pattern.

drape this soft, dusky-pink wrap around your shoulders anytime, anywhere, and it will instantly make you feel special, whether you wear it over a strappy dress on a chilly summer evening or wrapped around you while you're reading in bed or knitting. From the sweet detail of the narrow turned-down collar to the small cable twists, we love this wrap.

Cable Wrap   Debbie Bliss

MATERIALS
9(10) 1¾oz (50g) balls of Debbie Bliss Cashmerino DK, shade 16 Pale Pink
One Size 6 (4mm) circular knitting needle, 32 inches (80cm) long
One Size 5 (3.75mm) circular knitting needle, 32 inches (80cm) long
Cable needle
Large safety pin or brooch to fasten

MEASUREMENTS
To fit bust
32-36   38-42 inches
81-92   97-107cm
Actual size at lower edge
60   61½ inches
152   156cm
Length at center back
14½   15½ inches
36   39cm

GAUGE
22 sts and 30 rows = 4 inches (10cm) square measured over stockinette stitch using Size 6 needles or the size required to obtain the correct gauge.

ABBREVIATIONS
See page 129.
C4[6, 8]B Slip next 2[3, 4] sts onto cable needle and hold at back of work, K2[3, 4] from LHN, then K2[3, 4] from cable needle.
C4[6, 8]F Slip next 2[3, 4] sts onto cable needle and hold at front of work, K2[3, 4] from LHN, then K2[3, 4] from cable needle.
C4/2B Slip next 2 sts onto cable needle and hold at back of work, K2tog tbl from LHN, then K2tog from cable needle.
C4/2F Slip next 2 sts onto cable needle and hold at front of work, K2tog from LHN, then K2tog tbl from cable needle.
C6/4B Slip next 3 sts onto cable needle and hold at back of work, [K2tog tbl, K1] from LHN, then [K2tog, K1] from cable needle.

C6/4F Slip next 3 sts onto cable needle and hold at front of work, [K1, K2tog] from LHN, then [K1, K2tog tbl] from cable needle.
C8/6B Slip next 4 sts onto cable needle and hold at back of work, [K2, K2tog tbl] from LHN, then [K2tog, K2] from cable needle.
C8/6F Slip next 4 sts onto cable needle and hold at front of work, [K2, K2tog] from LHN, then [K2, K2tog tbl] from cable needle.
C10/8B [Slip next 3 sts onto cable needle and hold at back of work, K2 from LHN, then [K2tog tbl, K1] from cable needle] twice.
C10/8F [Slip next 2 sts onto cable needle and hold at front of work, [K2tog, K1] from LHN, then K2 from cable needle] twice.

NOTES
When short-row shaping, refer to the wrapping technique on page 133.

RIGHT HALF
Using a Size 6 circular needle, cast on 221(229) sts.
Row 1 (WS) [K4, P4] 1(2) times, [K7, P8, K7, P4, K7, P4] 5 times, K7, P8, K7, P4, K2.
Row 2 P2, [C4B, P7, C8B, P7, C4B, P7] 5 times, C4B, P7, C8B, P7, [C4B, P4] 1(2) times.
Rows 3, 5, and 7 Repeat row 1.
Row 4 P2, [K4, P7, K8, P7, K4, P7] 5 times, K4, P7, K8, P7, [K4, P4] 1(2) times.
Row 6 P2, [C4B, P7, K8, P7, C4B, P7] 5 times, C4B, P7, K8, P7, [C4B, P4] 1(2) times.
Row 8 Repeat row 4.
These 8 rows form the pattern.
Repeat rows 1-8 eight(nine) times, then repeat row 1 once.
73(81) rows worked in all.

Shape shoulder
Row 1 (RS) P2, [C4B, P7, C8B, P7, C4B, P7] 4 times, C4B, P2tog, P5, C8/6B, P5, P2tog, [C4B, P7] twice, C8B, P7, [C4B, P4] 1(2) times.
217(225) sts.

This page: See page 88 for Floral Bolster Cushion pattern.

Row 2 and every alternate row to row 26 (WS) P all purl sts and K all knit sts as they appear to maintain st-st cables and reverse st-st background.

Row 3 P2, [K4, P7, K8, P7, K4, P7] 4 times, K4, P6, K6, P6, [K4, P7] twice, K8, P7, [K4, P4] 1(2) times.

Row 5 P2, [C4B, P7, K8, P7, C4B, P7] 4 times, C4B, P6, K6, P6, [C4B, P7] twice, K8, P7, [C4B, P4] 1(2) times.

Row 7 P2, [K4, P7, K8, P7, K4, P7] 4 times, K4, P2tog, P4, C6B, P4, P2tog, [K4, P7] twice, K8, P7, [K4, P4] 1(2) times. 215(223) sts.

Row 9 P2, [C4B, P7, C8B, P7, C4B, P7] 4 times, C4B, P5, K6, P5, [C4B, P7] twice, C8B, P7, [C4B, P4] 1(2) times.

Row 11 P2, [K4, P7, K8, P7, K4, P7] 4 times, K4, P5, K6, P5, [K4, P7] twice, K8, P7, [K4, P4] 1(2) times.

Row 13 P2, [C4B, P7, K8, P7, C4B, P7] 4 times, C4B, P2tog, P3, C6/4B, P3, P2tog, [C4B, P7] twice, K8, P7, [C4B, P4] 1(2) times. 211(219) sts.

Row 15 P2, [K4, P7, K8, P7, K4, P7] 4 times, [K4, P4] twice, [K4, P7] twice, K8, P7, [K4, P4] 1(2) times.

Row 17 P2, [C4B, P7, C8B, P7, C4B, P7] 4 times, C4B, P2tog, P2, C4B, P2, P2tog, [C4B, P7] twice, C8B, P7, [C4B, P4] 1(2) times. 209(217) sts.

Row 19 P2, [K4, P7, K8, P7, K4, P7] 4 times, [K4, P3] twice, [K4, P7] twice, K8, P7, [K4, P4] 1(2) times.

Row 21 P2, [C4B, P7, K8, P7, C4B, P7] 4 times, C4B, P2tog, P1, C4B, P1, P2tog, [C4B, P7] twice, K8, P7, [C4B, P4] 1(2) times. 207(215) sts.

Row 23 P2, [K4, P7, K8, P7, K4, P7] 4 times, [K4, P2] twice, [K4, P7] twice, K8, P7, [K4, P4] 1(2) times.

Row 25 P2, [C4B, P7, C8B, P7, C4B, P7] 4 times, C4B, P2tog, C4/2B, P2tog, [C4B, P7] twice, C8B, P7, [C4B, P4] 1(2) times. 203(211) sts.

Row 27 P2, [K4, P7, K8, P7, K4, P7] 4 times, K3, ssk, K2, K2tog, K3, P7, K4, P7, K8, P7, [K4, P4] 1(2) times. 201(209) sts.

Row 28 (WS) [K4, P4] 1(2) times, K7, P8, K7, P4, K7, P10, [K7, P4, K7, P8, K7, P4] 4 times, K2.

Row 29 P2, [C4B, P7, K8, P7, C4B, P7] 4 times, C10/8B, P7, C4B, P7, K8, P7, [C4B, P4] 1(2) times. 199(207) sts.

Row 30 (WS) [K4, P4] 1(2) times, K7, P8, K7, P4, K7, P8, [K7, P4, K7, P8, K7, P4] 4 times, K2.

Row 31 P2, [K4, P7, K8, P7, K4, P7] 4 times, K8, P7, K4, P7, K8, P7, [K4, P4] 1(2) times.

Row 32 (WS) Repeat row 30.

Row 33 P2, [C4B, P7, C8B, P7, C4B, P7] 4 times, C8B, P7, C4B, P7, C8B, P7, [C4B, P4] 1(2) times.

Row 34 Repeat row 30.

Row 35 Bind off all sts, working [K1, K2tog, K1] across each 4-st cable and [K1, K2tog, K2, K2tog, K1] across each 8-st cable.

LEFT HALF

Using a Size 6 circular needle, cast on 221(229) sts.

Row 1 (WS) K2, [P4, K7, P8, K7, P4, K7] 5 times, P4, K7, P8, K7, [P4, K4] 1(2) times.

Row 2 [P4, C4F] 1(2) times, [P7, C8F, P7, C4F, P7, C4F] 5 times, P7, C8F, P7, C4F, P2.

Rows 3, 5, and 7 Repeat row 1.

Row 4 [P4, K4] 1(2) times, [P7, K8, P7, K4, P7, K4] 5 times, P7, K8, P7, K4, P2.

Row 6 [P4, C4F] 1(2) times, [P7, K8, P7, C4F, P7, C4F] 5 times, P7, K8, P7, C4F, P2.

Row 8 Repeat row 4.

These 8 rows form the pattern.
Repeat rows 1–8 eight(9) times, then repeat row 1 once.
73(81) rows worked in all.

Shape shoulder

Row 1 (RS) [P4, C4F] 1(2) times, P7, C8F, [P7, C4F] twice, P2tog, P5, C8/6F, P5, P2tog, C4F, [P7, C4F, P7, C8F, P7, C4F] 4 times, P2. 217(225) sts.

Row 2 and every alternate row to row 26 (WS) P all purl sts and K all knit sts as they appear to maintain st-st cables and reverse st-st background.

Row 3 [P4, K4] 1(2) times, P7, K8, [P7, K4] twice, P6, K6, P6, K4, [P7, K4, P7, K8, P7, K4] 4 times, P2.

Row 5 [P4, C4F] 1(2) times, P7, K8, [P7, C4F] twice, P6, K6, P6, C4F, [P7, C4F, P7, K8, P7, C4F] 4 times, P2.

Row 7 [P4, K4] 1(2) times, P7, K8, [P7, K4] twice, P2tog, P4, C6F, P4, P2tog, K4, [P7, K4, P7, K8, P7, K4] 4 times, P2. 215(223) sts.

Row 9 [P4, C4F] 1(2) times, P7, C8F, [P7, C4F] twice, P5, K6, P5, C4F, [P7, C4F, P7, C8F, P7, C4F] 4 times, P2.

Row 11 [P4, K4] 1(2) times, P7, K8, [P7, K4] twice, P5, K6, P5, K4, [P7, K4, P7, K8, P7, K4] 4 times, P2.

Row 13 [P4, C4F] 1(2) times, P7, K8, [P7, C4F] twice, P2tog, P3, C6/4F, P3, P2tog, C4F, [P7, C4F, P7, K8, P7, C4F] 4 times, P2. 211(219) sts.

Row 15 [P4, K4] 1(2) times, P7, K8, [P7, K4] twice, [P4, K4] twice, [P7, K4, P7, K8, P7, K4] 4 times, P2.

Row 17 [P4, C4F] 1(2) times, P7, C8F, [P7, C4F] twice, P2tog, P2, C4F, P2, P2tog, C4F, [P7, C4F, P7, C8F, P7, C4F] 4 times, P4. 209(217) sts.

Row 19 [P4, K4] 1(2) times, P7, K8, [P7, K4] twice, [P3, K4] twice, [P7, K4, P7, K8, P7, K4] 4 times, P2.

Row 21 [P4, C4F] 1(2) times, P7, K8, [P7, C4F] twice, P2tog, P1, C4F, P1, P2tog, C4F, [P7, C4F, P7, K8, P7, C4F] 4 times, P2. 207(215) sts.

Row 23 [P4, K4] 1(2) times, P7, K8, [P7, K4] twice, [P2, K4] twice, [P7, K4, P7, K8, P7, K4] 4 times, P2.

Row 25 [P4, C4F] 1(2) times, P7, C8F, [P7, C4F] twice, P2tog, C4/2F, P2tog, C4F, [P7, C4F, P7, C8F, P7, C4F] 4 times, P2. 203(211) sts.

Row 27 [P4, K4] 1(2) times, P7, K8, P7, K4, P7, K3, ssk, K2, K2tog, K3, [P7, K4, P7, K8, P7, K4] 4 times, P2. 201(209) sts.

Row 28 (WS) K2, [P4, K7, P8, K7, P4, K7] 4 times, P10, K7, P4, K7, P8, K7, [P4, K4] 1(2) times.

Row 29 [P4, C4F] 1(2) times, P7, K8, P7, C4F, P7, C10/8F, [P7, C4F, P7, K8, P7, C4F] 4 times, P2. 199(207) sts.

Row 30 (WS) K2, [P4, K7, P8, K7, P4, K7] 4 times, P8, K7, P4, K7, P8, K7, [P4, K4] 1(2) times.

Row 31 [P4, K4] 1(2) times, P7, K8, P7, K4, P7, K8, [P7, K4, P7, K8, P7, K4] 4 times, P2.

Row 32 (WS) Repeat row 30.

Row 33 [P4, C4F] 1(2) times, P7, C8F, P7, C4F, P7, C8F, [P7, C4F, P7, C8F, P7, C4F] 4 times, P2.

Row 34 Repeat row 30.

Row 35 Bind off all sts, working [K1, K2tog, K1] across each 4-st cable and [K1, K2tog tbl, K2, K2tog tbl, K1] across each 8 st cable.

COLLAR

Block each piece following the instructions on page 138 and referring to the yarn label.

Join back seam.

With right side facing and using a Size 5 circular needle, pick up and knit 137 sts along bound-off edge to center of first shaped cable, then pick up and knit 65(77) sts to center of second shaped cable, then pick up and knit 137 sts to end. 339(351) sts.

Row 1 (WS) Knit.

Row 2 (RS) Knit to last 160(166) sts, turn.

Row 3 Sl1, K20, turn.

Row 4 Sl1, K22, turn.

Row 5 Sl1, K24, turn.

Row 6 Sl1, K26, turn.

Cont working short rows in this way, working 2 more sts on every row until the row 'Sl1, K88, turn' has been worked.

Next row (RS) Sl1, K92, turn.

Next row Sl1, K96, turn.

Cont working short rows in this way, working 4 more sts on every row until the row "Sl1, K128, turn" has been worked.

Next row Sl1, K136, turn.

Cont working short rows in this way, working 8 more sts on every row until the row "Sl1, K176, turn" has been worked.

Next row Sl1, knit to end.

Next row Using a Size 6 needle, bind off 90(96) sts knitwise, bind off next 159(159) sts purlwise, then bind off rem 90(96) sts knitwise.

FINISHING

Fold the wider part of the collar over onto the right side. To wear, wrap around your shoulders with the shaped cables on your shoulders and fasten with a pin or gorgeous brooch.

b ed socks may not be the most seductive articles of clothing to wear in the boudoir, but your feet will thank you for them on chilly nights, and they're great to wear around the home instead of slippers. The super-soft socks with a flirty lace ruffle are the ideal pattern to use divine pure cashmere yarn, as they require only a small quantity. There's nothing better to spoil your feet with, and you'll never want to take them off.

Lace Ruffle Bed Socks   Leslie Scanlon

MATERIALS
Two 2oz (55g) skeins Jade Sapphire 6-ply DK Mongolian
  Cashmere, shade 65 Silver Fox
Set of Size 3 (3.25mm) double-pointed needles
Set of Size 4 (3.5mm) double-pointed needles
Set of Size 5 (3.75mm) double-pointed needles
Set of Size 7 (4.5mm) double-pointed needles
Stitch markers
Tapestry needle

MEASUREMENTS
Shoe/Sock size

S	M	L
5–6	7–8	9–10

Foot length
9 inches (23cm)   9½ inches (24cm)   10 inches (15.5cm)
The foot length is adjustable.

GAUGE
22 sts and 30 rows = 4 inches (10cm) square measured over stockinette stitch on Size 3 needles or the size required to obtain the correct gauge.

ABBREVIATIONS
See page 129.

NOTES
When making a yo after a knit stitch and before a purl stitch, bring the yarn to the front between the needles, then over the top of the RHN and back to the front (also known as "yarn round needle").
When making a yo after a purl stitch and before a knit stitch, take the yarn to the back between the needles, then over the top of the RHN and between the needles to the back again.

SOCK (Make 2)
Using Size 5 double-pointed needles, cast on 40(44, 48) sts evenly onto 3 needles.
Join for knitting in the round and PM at the beginning of the round.
Round 1 * K1, P1; rep from * to end.
Repeating this round forms K1, P1 rib.
Cont rib until sock measures 3(3½, 4) inches/7.5(9, 10)cm.

Divide for heel and instep
Knit to the marker then K10(12, 12) sts after the marker. The 10(12, 12) sts before the marker and the 10(12, 12) sts after the marker are the 20(24, 24) sts for the heel.
Divide the rem 20(20, 24) sts evenly onto 2 needles for the instep.

Using Size 3(3, 4) double-pointed needles, work the heel sts back and forth as follows:
Row 1 (WS) Sl1P, purl to end.
Row 2 (RS) Sl1K, * K1, sl1K; rep from * to last st, K1.
Rep rows 1 and 2 nine(10, 12) times, ending with a RS row. 20(22, 24) rows worked.

Turn the heel
Row 1 (WS) Sl1P, P11(13, 13), P2tog tbl, P1, turn.
Row 2 Sl1K, K5, K2tog tbl, K1, turn.
Row 3 Sl1P, purl to 1 st before previous turn, P2tog tbl, P1, turn.
Row 4 Sl1K, knit to 1 st before previous turn, K2tog tbl, K1, turn.
Repeat rows 3 and 4 until all sts have been worked, ending with a row 4 and omitting the P1 at the end of the penultimate row and the K1 at the end of the last row. 12(14, 14) sts.

Form the gusset

Place half of the remaining heel sts onto another Size 3(3, 5) double-pointed needle and, using the same needle, with RS facing, pick up and knit 10(11, 12) slipped sts along the side of the heel. Combine the 20(20, 24) sts for the instep from the next 2 double-pointed needles onto another Size 3(3, 5) double-pointed needle and knit these sts. With a third Size 3(3, 5) double-pointed needle, pick up and knit 10(11, 12) slipped sts along the other side of the heel. On the same double-pointed needle, knit the remaining half of the heel sts (this is now the center back of the heel). 52(56, 62) sts.

Resume knitting in the round. Join and PM at the beginning of the round.

Round 1 Knit.

Round 2 On first needle, knit to last 3 sts, K2tog, K1; on second needle, knit all sts; on third needle K1, ssk, knit to end.

Repeat rounds 1 and 2 until 40(44, 48) sts rem.

Cont working straight in the round until the sock measures 7¼(7¾, 8) inches/18.5(19.5, 21)cm or 1¾ inches (4.5cm) less than the desired length, measuring from the back of the heel to the tip of the big toe.

Shape toe

Round 1 On first needle, knit to last 3 sts, K2tog, K1; on second needle, K1, ssk, knit to last 2 sts, K2tog, K1; on third needle, K1, ssk, knit to end.

Round 2 Knit.

Repeat rounds 1 and 2 until 12(16, 20) sts rem.

Join toe

Kitchener-stitch/graft the toe together as follows (see pages 139-40):

Small size and Large size

K3(5) sts from first needle to fourth (empty) needle and slip 3(5) sts from third needle to the other end of the fourth needle. The first and third needles are now empty. There are now 6(10) sts on both the second and fourth needles.

Medium size

K4 sts from first needle to fourth (empty) needle and slip 4 sts from third needle to the other end of the fourth needle. Slip last st on first needle to second needle and the remaining stitch on the third needle to the other end of the second needle. The first and third needles are now empty. There are now 8 sts on both the second and fourth needles.

All sizes

Holding the 2 needles parallel, with a threaded tapestry needle, * go into the first st on the front needle as if to knit and pull the st off the needle, then go into the next st on the front needle as if to purl and leave this st on the needle. Now go into the first st on the back needle as if to purl and pull this st off the needle, then go into the second st on the back needle as if to knit and leave that st on the needle.

Repeat from * until 1 st remains on each needle. Weave yarn through rem sts and secure on the wrong side.

RUFFLE

With the RS facing, using Size 4 needles and starting at the center back of the rib, pick up 40(44, 48) sts all round.

Change to Size 7 needles and work back and forth as follows:

Row 1 (WS of ruffle, RS of sock) * K3, P1; rep from * to end. 40(44, 48) sts.

Row 2 K1, * P3, K1, rep from * to last 3 sts, P3.

Row 3 K3, * yo, P1, yo, K3; rep from * to last st, P1. 58(64, 70) sts.

Row 4 K1, * P3, K3; rep from * to last 3 sts, end P3.

Row 5 K3, * yo, P3, yo, K3; rep from * to last st, P1. 76(84, 92) sts.

Row 6 K1, * P3, K5; rep from * to last 3 sts, P3.

Row 7 K3, * yo, P5, yo, K3; rep from * to last st, P1. 94(104, 114) sts.

Row 8 K1, * P3, K7; rep from * to last 3 sts, P3.

Row 9 K1, * yo, K2tog tbl; rep from * to last st, P1. 94(104, 114) sts.

Row 10 Knit.

Bind off.

FINISHING

Join ruffle seam.

Weave in all ends.

Block each piece following the instructions on page 138 and referring to the yarn label. Or, with a press cloth, gently block the ruffle by spreading it out flat a small amount at a time.

This pretty floral throw will have you yearning for more lounging time. It is super-cozy as well as beautiful, and would be a welcome extra layer on the bed on chilly nights or make a great throw to snuggle under in front of the TV. You can make it as large as you like by adding more squares, and you can play around with the configuration of the flowers and leaves, either attaching them at regular intervals on the blanket or scattering them over its surface in random clusters.

Flower Posy Throw   Nicki Trench

MATERIALS

Sixteen 1¾oz (50g) balls of Rowan Pure Wool DK, shade 001 Clay (Yarn A)

One 1¾oz (50g) ball Rowan Pure Wool DK, shade 025 Tea Rose (Yarn B)

One 1¾oz (50g) ball Rowan Pure Wool DK, shade 032 Gilt (Yarn C)

One 1¾oz (50g) ball Rowan Pure Wool DK, shade 019 Avocado (Yarn D)

One 1¾oz (50g) ball Rowan Pure Wool DK, shade 026 Hyacinth

One 1¾oz (50g) ball Rowan Pure Wool DK, shade 027 Hydrangea

One 1¾oz (50g) ball Rowan Pure Wool DK, shade 028 Raspberry

One 1¾oz (50g) ball Rowan Pure Wool DK, shade 029 Pomegranate

Pair Size 6 (4mm) knitting needles, 14 inches (35cm) long

One Size 6 (4mm) circular needle, 24 inches (60cm) long (optional)

Pair Size 5 (3.5mm) knitting needles

Row counter

MEASUREMENTS

Length including edging approximately 53 inches (135cm)

Width including edging approximately 41 inches (105cm)

Each square 12 x 12 inches (30 x 30cm)

GAUGE

22 sts and 30 rows = 4 inches (10cm) square measured over stockinette stitch using Rowan Pure Wool DK on Size 6 needles or the size required to obtain the correct gauge.

ABBREVIATIONS

See page 129.

NOTES

For the top and bottom edgings, the stitches will fit, but with a tight squeeze, onto Size 6 14-inch- (35cm-) long straight needles. You may find it easier to use a Size 6 24-inch- (60cm-) long circular needle and work back and forth.

After the flowers have been sewn in place, the seams of the throw can be hidden by working mattress stitch (see pages 138–39) up the vertical seams and working duplicate stitch over the horizontal seams (see page 140).

SQUARES FOR THROW (Make 12)

Using Size 6 needles and Yarn A, cast on 66 sts.

Beg with a knit row, work 90 rows st-st.

Bind off.

Join the squares

Block each square following the instructions on page 138 and referring to the yarn label.

Join squares with backstitch to make one large rectangle, 3 squares across and 4 squares down.

When joining the squares, the 3 squares at the top and the 3 squares at the bottom must have the bound-off edges at the outer edge of the throw, ready for picking up stitches for the edgings.

TOP EDGING

Using Size 6 needles and Yarn A, pick up and knit 193 sts evenly across the top of the throw.

Row 1 Sl1, * K1, P1, rep from * to end.

Row 2 Sl1, M1, * K1, P1, rep from * to last 2 sts, K1, M1, K1. 195 sts.

Row 3 Sl1, * P1, K1; rep from * to end.

Row 4 Sl1, M1, * P1, K1; rep from * to last st 2 sts, P1, M1, P1. 197 sts.
Repeating these 4 rows forms seed stitch with corner shaping.
Repeat rows 1–4 six times. 221 sts.
Bind off in seed stitch.

BOTTOM EDGING
Work as for top edging.

SIDE EDGING (Make 2)
Increasing side edging
Using Size 6 needles and Yarn A, cast on 2 sts.

Row 1 (WS) K1, P1.
Row 2 Sl1, M1, K1. 3 sts.
Row 3 Sl1, P1, K1.
Row 4 Sl1, M1, P1, K1. 4 sts.
Row 5 Sl1, P1, K1, P1.
Row 6 Sl1, M1, K1, P1, K1. 5 sts.
Row 7 Sl1, P1, K1, P1, K1.
Row 8 Sl1, M1, [P1, K1] twice. 6 sts.
Row 9 Sl1, P1, [K1, P1] twice.
Row 10 Sl1, M1, * K1, P1; rep from * to last st, K1. 7 sts.
Row 11 Sl1, * P1, K1; rep from * to end.

Row 12 Sl1, M1, * P1, K1; rep from * to end. 8 sts.

Row 13 Sl1, * P1, K1; rep from * to last st, P1.

Repeat rows 10–13 four times, then rows 10 and 11 once. 17 sts.

Main part of side edging

Next row Sl1, * P1, K1; rep from * to end.

Next row Sl1, * P1, K1; rep from * to end.

Repeating these 2 rows forms seed stitch.

Repeat these 2 rows for another 358 rows or until the narrower edge of the main part of the side edging, when slightly stretched, fits along the side of the throw to the bound-off edge of the 4th square, ending at the narrower edge.

Decreasing side edging

Row 1 Sl1, K2tog, * P1, K1; rep from * to end. 16 sts.

Row 2 Sl1, * P1, K1; rep from * to last st, P1.

Row 3 Sl1, P2tog, * K1, P1; rep from * to last st, K1. 15 sts.

Row 4 Sl1, * P1, K1; rep from * to end.

Repeat rows 1–4 until 2 sts remain.

Next row K2tog.

Fasten off.

Join the edgings to the throw

Block each edging following the instructions on page 138 and referring to the yarn label.

Attach side edgings to the throw with mattress stitch (see pages 138–39).

Join the corners of the side edgings to the corners of the top and bottom edgings with mattress stitch.

FLOWERS

Large roses (Make 24 in various shades of pink Rowan Pure Wool DK)

Using Size 5 needles, cast on 10 sts.

Row 1 (RS) Knit.

Rows 2, 4, and 6 Purl.

Row 3 Knit into front and back of every st. 20 sts.

Row 5 Knit into front and back of every st. 40 sts.

Row 7 Knit into front and back of every st. 80 sts.

Row 8 Purl.

Bind off.

Twist rose into spiral and sew at back to hold in place.

Small roses (Make 60 in various shades of pink Rowan Pure Wool DK and Yarn C)

Using Size 5 needles, cast on 21 sts.

Rows 1–3 Knit.

Pass all sts one at a time over the first stitch until all stitches are off the RHN except first st.

Fasten off.

Central flowers (Make 12 using Yarn B)

Using Size 5 needles and Yarn B, cast on 5 sts.

Row 1 Knit into front and back of every st. 10 sts.

Rows 2 and 4 Purl.

Row 3 Knit into front and back of every st. 20 sts.

Row 5 Bind off 1 st, * slip st from RHN to LHN needle, cast on 3 sts, bind off 5 sts; rep from * until 1 st remains.

Fasten off.

Using Yarn C, embroider 3 or 5 French knots in the center of the flower (see page 137).

Leaves (Make 60 using Yarn D)

Using Size 5 needles and Yarn D, cast on 5 sts.

Row 1 (RS) K2, yo, K1, yo, K2. 7 sts.

Row 2 and every alternate row Purl.

Row 3 K3, yo, K1, yo, K3. 9 sts.

Row 5 K4, yo, K1, yo, K4. 11 sts.

Row 7 Ssk, K7, K2tog. 9 sts.

Row 9 Ssk, K5, K2tog. 7 sts.

Row 11 Ssk, K3, K2tog. 5 sts.

Row 13 Ssk, K1, K2tog. 3 sts.

Row 15 Sl1, K2tog, psso. 1 st.

Fasten off.

FINISHING

Sew a central flower at the center of each square of the throw.

Sew three small roses in various shades around the central flower and sew three leaves between the small roses.

Sew three large roses of various shades, bunched together, in each corner on the edging of the throw. Sew three leaves between each rose.

Sew three large roses bunched together at the center of the edging between each corner. Sew three leaves between each rose.

Sew three small roses between each group of large roses around the edging.

feminine fripperies

You can make this gorgeous wrap in either a narrow or wide version, and decorate the lacy edging with ribbon, beads, sequins, or buttons. Draped over the end of a bed or the back of a sofa or chair, it will bring a feminine touch to any room. The fine alpaca yarn is very light but hangs beautifully and feels soft and cozy when wrapped around you.

Scallop-Edged Lace Wrap   Kate Samphier

MATERIALS
8(16) 1¾oz (50g) skeins Blue Sky Alpacas Sportweight, shade 528
   Vivid Lilac
Pair Size 8 (5mm) knitting needles
Four 27(55)-inch- (70(140)cm-) lengths of pink silk or taffeta ribbon,
   1¼ inches (3cm) wide
Pink bugle beads and sequins to decorate

MEASUREMENTS
Width

14	27½ inches
35.5	70.5cm

Length

67	67 inches
170	170cm

GAUGE
20 sts and 30 rows = 4 inches (10cm) square over garter-stripe pattern using Size 8 needles or the size required to obtain the correct gauge.

ABBREVIATIONS
See page 129.

NOTES
The number of stitches changes over the rows.

The wrap/throw is made in two panels, which are grafted together.

WRAP/THROW (Make 2)

Using Size 8 needles, cast on 93(184) sts.

Work 12 rows in scallop-edge pattern, as follows.

Row 1 (RS) K3, * skpo, sl2, K3tog, p2sso, K2tog, K4; rep from * to last 12 sts, skpo, sl2, K3tog, p2sso, K2tog, K3. 51(100) sts.

Row 2 P4, * yo, P1, yo, P6; rep from * to last 5 sts, yo, P1, yo, P4. 65(128) sts.

Row 3 K1, yo, * K2, skpo, K1, K2tog, K2, yo; rep from * to last st, K1. 59(115) sts.

Row 4 P2, * yo, P2, yo, P3, yo, P2, yo, P1; rep from * to last st, P1. 87(171) sts.

Row 5 K2, yo, K1, * yo, skpo, K1, sl1, K2tog, psso, K1, K2tog, [yo, K1] 3 times; rep from * to last 12 sts, yo, skpo, K1, sl1, K2tog, psso, K1, K2tog, yo, K1, yo, K2. 87(171) sts.

Row 6 Purl. 87(171) sts.

Row 7 K5, * yo, sl2, K3tog, p2sso, yo, K7; rep from * to last 10 sts, yo, sl2, K3tog, p2sso, yo, K5. 73(143) sts.

Rows 8–11 Knit. 73(143) sts.

Row 12 (WS) Purl, inc 0(2) sts evenly across the row. 73(145) sts.

Work 10 rows in eyelet-chevron pattern, as follows.

Row 1 (RS) K4, * K2tog, yo, K1, yo, skpo, K7; rep from * to last 9 sts, K2tog, yo, K1, yo, skpo, K4. 73(145) sts.

Rows 2, 4, 6, and 8 Purl.

Row 3 K3, * K2tog, yo, K3, yo, skpo, K5; rep from * to last 10 sts, K2tog, yo, K3, yo, skpo, K3.

Row 5 K2, * K2tog, yo, K5, yo, skpo, K3; rep from * to last 11 sts, K2tog, yo, K5, yo, skpo, K2.

Row 7 K1, * K2tog, yo, K7, yo, skpo, K1; rep from * to end.

Row 9 K2tog, yo, K9, * yo, sl1, K2tog, psso, yo, K9; rep from * to last 2 sts, yo, skpo.

Row 10 (WS) Purl.

Next row (RS) Knit, decreasing 4 sts evenly across the row. 69(141) sts.

Work 3 rows in ribbon-eyelet pattern, as follows.

Row 1 (WS) Knit.

Row 2 P1, * yo, P2tog; rep from * to end.

Row 3 Knit.

Work 13 rows in diamond and eyelet pattern, as follows.

Row 1 (RS) Knit.

Rows 2, 4, 6, 8, 10, and 12 Purl.

Row 3 * K4, yo, skpo; rep from * to last 3 sts, K3.

Row 5 K2, * K2tog, yo, K1, yo, skpo, K1; rep from * to last st, K1.

Row 7 K1, K2tog, yo, * K3, yo, sl1, K2tog, psso, yo; rep from * to last 6 sts, K3, yo, skpo, K1.

Row 9 K3, * yo, sl1, K2tog, psso, yo, K3; rep from * to end.

Row 11 Repeat row 3.

Row 13 (RS) Knit.

Work 3 rows in ribbon-eyelet pattern, as follows.

Row 1 (WS) Knit.

Row 2 P1, * yo, P2tog; rep from * to end.

Row 3 Knit.

Next row (RS) Knit, increasing 2(0) sts evenly across row. 71(141) sts.

Next row Purl.

Work 28 rows wide leaf border pattern, as follows.

Rows 1 (RS) and 2 Purl.

Row 3 K5, * K2tog, [K1, yo, K1] in next st, ssk, K9; rep from * to end, ending last rep K5 instead of K9.

Row 4 K5, * P5, K9; rep from * to end, ending last rep K5 instead of K9.

Row 5 K4, * K2tog, [K1, yo] twice, K1, ssk, K7; rep from * to end, ending last rep K4 instead of K7.

Row 6 K4, * P7, K7; rep from * to end, ending last rep K4 instead of K7.

Row 7 K3, * K2tog, K2, yo, K1, yo, K2, ssk, K5; rep from * to end, ending last rep K3 instead of K5.

Row 8 K3, * P9, K5; rep from * to end, ending last rep K3 instead of K5.

Row 9 K2, * K2tog, K3, yo, K1, yo, K3, ssk, K3; rep from * to end, ending last rep K2 instead of K3.

Row 10 K2, * P11, K3; rep from * to end, ending last rep, K2 instead of K3.

Row 11 K1, * K2tog, K4, yo, K1, yo, K4, ssk, K1; rep from * to end.

Row 12 K1, * P13, K1; rep from * to end.

Row 13 K1, * ssk, [K3, yo] twice, K3, K2tog, K1; rep from * to end.

Row 14 Repeat row 12.

Row 15 K1, * yo, ssk, K3, yo, sl1, K2tog, psso, yo, K3, K2tog, yo, K1; rep from * to end.

Row 16 Repeat row 10.

Row 17 K2, * yo, ssk, K7, K2tog, yo, K3; rep from * to end, ending last repeat K2 instead of K3.

Row 18 Repeat row 8.

Row 19 K3, * yo, ssk, K5, K2tog, yo, K5; rep from * to end, ending last repeat, K3 instead of K5.

Row 20 Repeat row 6.

Row 21 K4, * yo, ssk, K3, K2tog, yo, K7; rep from * to end, ending last rep K4 instead of K7.

Row 22 Repeat row 4.

Row 23 K5, * yo, ssk, K1, K2tog, yo, K9; rep from * to end, ending last repeat K5 instead of K9.

Row 24 K6, * P3, K11; rep from * to end, ending last rep K6 instead of K11.

Row 25 K6, * yo, sl2, K1, p2sso, yo, K11; rep from * to end, ending last rep K6 instead of K11.

Row 26 Purl.

Rows 27 and 28 Knit.

Work 4 rows in garter-ridge pattern, as follows.

Row 1 (RS) Knit.

Row 2 Purl.

Row 3 Knit.

Row 4 Knit.

Repeat rows 1-4 until wrap/throw measures 33½ inches (85cm) from cast-on edge.

Leave these 71(141) sts on a holder.

Work second panel as above, ending on row 3 instead of row 4 of garter-ridge pattern repeat.

FINISHING

Block each piece following the instructions on page 138 and referring to the yarn label.

Kitchener-stitch/graft the two panels together and press gently with a warm iron (see pages 139-40).

Randomly sew beads and sequins between the ribbon-eyelet panels and along the scallop edge on both ends of the wrap/throw.

Thread ribbon through ribbon eyelet panels and secure at each end.

*f*lowers are a favorite motif for feminine interiors, and a large pink bloom brings a sense of delicacy and fragility to this knitted cushion cover with a matching fluted border. Three layers of petals, crafted from light-as-air Rowan Kidsilk Haze in different shades of deep raspberry and pale pink, are sewn together and decorated with chain-stitch embroidery and pearl beads, then sewn to the center of the cushion cover.

Flower Cushion Cover   Nicki Trench

MATERIALS
Three 1¾oz (50g) balls Rowan Kid Classic, shade 851 Straw (Yarn A)
One 1¾oz (50g) ball Rowan Kidsilk Haze, shade 583 Blushes (Yarn B)
One 1¾oz (50g) ball Rowan Kidsilk Haze, shade 630 Fondant (Yarn C)
Small amount of smooth yarn or embroidery yarn for stamens
Pair each Size 6 (4mm) and 8 (5mm) knitting needles
Row counter
6 small pearl beads, approximately 4-5mm diameter
5 snap fasteners
Tapestry needle
Beading needle

MEASUREMENTS
16 x 16 inches (40 x 40cm) square without edging

GAUGE
19 sts and 25 rows = 4 inches (10cm) square measured over stockinette stitch using Kid Classic (Yarn A) and Size 8 needles or the size required to obtain the correct gauge.

ABBREVIATIONS
See page 129.

CUSHION COVER
Using Size 8 needles and Yarn A, cast on 76 sts.
Row 1 (RS) Knit.
Row 2 Purl.
Repeating these 2 rows forms stockinette stitch.
Repeat rows 1 and 2 twice.
Row 7 Knit.
Row 8 (WS) (first fold line) Knit.
Rows 9-104 Beginning with a knit row, work 96 rows st-st.

Rows 105-108 (center fold line) Knit.
Rows 109-204 Beginning with a knit row, work 96 rows st-st.
Row 205 Knit.
Row 206 (WS) (third fold line) Knit.
Rows 207-212 Beginning with a knit row, work 6 rows in st-st ending with a purl row.
Bind off.

Cushion side edgings (Make 2)
Using Size 8 needles and Yarn A, with RS facing, pick up and knit 202 sts along whole length of side edge.
Bind off all stitches knitwise.

FINISHING
Block the cover following the instructions on page 138 and referring to the yarn label.
Fold the cushion cover in half with WS facing each other and the first and third fold lines meeting at the top. Join side seams with mattress stitch (see pages 138-39).
Fold the first and third fold lines to the WS so the garter-stitch row creates the top edge of the cushion and slipstitch the cast-on and bound-off edges on the inside.
Attach snap fasteners.

FLOWER (Make 1)
Outer petal
Using Size 6 needles and Yarn B, cast on 9 sts.
Row 1 K4, yo, K5. 10 sts.
Rows 2, 4, 6, 8, 10, 12, 14, and 16 Knit.
Row 3 K4, yo, K6. 11 sts.
Row 5 K4, yo, K7. 12 sts.
Row 7 K4, yo, K8. 13 sts.

Row 9 K4, yo, K9. 14 sts.
Row 11 K4, yo, K10. 15 sts.
Row 13 K4, yo, K11. 16 sts.
Row 15 K4, yo, K12. 17 sts.
Row 17 K4, yo, K13. 18 sts.
Row 18 Bind off 9 sts, knit to end. 9 sts.
Repeat rows 1–18 five times, binding off all sts on the 18th row of the last repeat.
Join bound-off edge to cast-on edge. Weave yarn in and out of center stitches, pull tight, and secure.

Large inner petal

Using Size 6 needles and Yarn C, cast on 6 sts.
Row 1 K3, yo, K3. 7 sts.
Rows 2, 4, 6, 8, 10, 12, and 14 rows Knit.
Row 3 K3, yo, K4. 8 sts.
Row 5 K3, yo, K5. 9 sts.
Row 7 K3, yo, K6. 10 sts.
Row 9 K3, yo, K7. 11 sts.
Row 11 K3, yo, K8. 12 sts.
Row 13 K3, yo, K9. 13 sts.
Row 15 K3, yo, K10. 14 sts.
Row 16 Bind off 7sts, knit to end. 7 sts.
Repeat rows 1–16 five times, binding off all sts on the 16th row of the last repeat.
Join bound-off edge to cast-on edge. Weave yarn in and out of center stitches, pull tight, and secure.

Small inner petal

Using Size 6 needles and Yarn B, cast on 5 sts.
Row 1 K2, yo, K3. 6 sts.
Rows 2, 4, 6, and 8 Knit
Row 3 K2, yo, K4. 7 sts.
Row 5 K2, yo, K5. 8 sts.
Row 7 K2, yo, K6. 9 sts.
Row 9 K2, yo, K7. 10 sts.
Row 10 Bind off 5 sts, knit to end. 5 sts.
Repeat rows 1–10 five times, binding off all sts on the 10th row of the last repeat.
Join bound-off edge to cast-on edge. Weave yarn in and out of center stitches, pull tight, and secure.

FINISHING

Sew the smaller petals over the larger petals and secure in place as one big flower.
Using a tapestry needle, embroider 6 stamens in chain stitch (5 small chains per stamen), starting from the center of the flower to halfway up the middle of each small center inner petal (see page 138). When the fifth small chain on each stamen has been completed, use the beading needle to thread one bead and attach it to the top of the stamen.
Sew the flower onto the center of the cushion cover.

EDGING

Using Size 6 needles and Yarn B, cast on 9 sts.
Repeat rows 1–18 of the pattern given for the outer petal of the flower 24 times, binding off all sts on the 18th row of the last repeat.
Sew in place around the outside edge of the cushion, 6 points on each of the 4 sides.

V arious stitches and yarns have been used to create this luscious circular floor cushion, made of different-textured segments in mouthwatering shades of orange, pink, lilac, and blue. This is a great way to try your hand at new stitches, such as broken rib and blackberry, and it is also a chance to experiment with color or use up spare balls of yarn.

Circular Floor Cushion   Nicky Thomson

MATERIALS
Two 3½oz (100g) skeins Manos del Uruguay, shade 2624 (Yarn A)
Two 1¾oz (50g) skeins Blue Sky Alpacas Alpaca Silk, shade 129
    Amethyst (Yarn B)
Two 3½oz (100g) skeins Manos del Uruguay, shade 2458 (Yarn C)
Two 1¾oz (50g) skeins Blue Sky Alpacas Alpaca Silk, shade 130
    Mandarin (Yarn D)
Two 3½oz (100g) skeins Manos del Uruguay, shade 2148 (Yarn E)
Two 3½oz (100g) skeins Noro Kochoran, shade 36 (Yarn F)
Pair Size 8 (5mm) knitting needles
Small amount of fiberfill for central knitted ball
Pillow form, 22 inches (55cm) diameter and 6 inches (15cm) deep
Tapestry needle

MEASUREMENTS
20 inches (51cm) diameter; 5 inches (12.5cm)

GAUGE
22 sts and 32 rows (16 ridges) = 4 inches (10cm) square measured over garter stitch using two strands of Blue Sky Alpacas Alpaca Silk on Size 8 needles or the size required to obtain the correct gauge.
22 sts and 24 rows = 4 inches (10cm) square measured over blackberry stitch using Manos del Uruguay on Size 8 needles or the size required to obtain the correct gauge.
20 sts and 24 rows = 4 inches (10cm) square measured over broken-rib stitch using Manos del Uruguay on Size 8 needles or the size required to obtain the correct gauge.
24 sts and 24 rows = 4 inches (10cm) square measured over broken-basket stitch using Noro Kochoran on Size 8 needles or the size required to obtain the correct gauge.

ABBREVIATIONS
See page 129.

TOP (5 triangular sections)

Section 1

Using Size 8 needles and two strands of Yarn B, cast on 4 sts.

Row 1 Knit.

Rows 2–3 Knit, inc one st at both ends of row. 8 sts.

Row 4 Knit.

Row 5 Knit, inc one st at both ends of row. 10 sts.

Row 6 Knit.

Repeat rows 5 and 6 to 60 stitches.

Bind off 6 stitches at beg of the next 10 rows.

Section 2

Repeat section 1 using Yarn D.

Section 3

Section 3 is worked in blackberry stitch. The basic stitch pattern is as follows:

Row 1 (RS) Purl.

Row 2 * [K1, P1, K1] into next stitch, P3tog; rep from * to end.

Row 3 Purl.

Row 4 * P3tog, [K1, P1, K1] into next stitch; rep from * to end.

The [K1. P1, K1] into next stitch is worked over the previous P3tog, and the P3tog is worked over the previous [K1. P1, K1] into next stitch.

Rows 1–4 form the pattern.

One stitch is increased at both ends of every alternate row while at the same time maintaining the continuity of the blackberry-stitch pattern. The extra "[K1, P1, K1] into next stitch" at the end of every alternate row makes 4 extra stitches.

Using Size 8 needles and Yarn A, cast on 5 stitches.

Row 1 and every alternate row (RS) Purl.

Row 2 (WS) Inc in first st, [K1, P1, K1] into next st, K1, inc in next st, K1. 9 sts.

Row 4 Inc in first st, K1, [K1, P1, K1] into next st, P3tog, [K1, P1, K1] into next st, inc in next st, K1. 13 sts.

Row 6 Inc in first stitch, K1, [[K1, P1, K1] into next st, P3tog] twice, [K1, P1, K1] into next st, inc in next st, K1. 17 sts.

Row 8 Inc in first st, K1, [[K1, P1, K1] into next st, P3tog] 3 times, [K1, P1, K1] into next st, inc in next st, K1. 21 sts.

Row 10 Inc in first stitch, K1, [[K1, P1, K1] into next st, P3tog] 4 times, [K1, P1, K1] into next st, knit to last 2 sts, inc in next st, K1. 25 sts.

Cont in blackberry stitch, inc one st at each end of every alternate row until row 38 has been worked. 81 sts (18 rows of blackberries).

Bind off 8 sts at beg of next 9 rows. 9 sts.

Bind off remaining stitches.

Section 4

Section 4 is worked in broken-rib stitch. The basic stitch pattern is as follows:

Row 1 K1, * P1, K1; rep from * to end.
Row 2 P1, *K1, P1; rep from * to end.
Rows 3 and 4 Knit.
These 4 rows form the pattern.

One stitch is increased at both ends of every alternate row while at the same time maintaining the continuity of the broken-rib-stitch pattern.

Using Size 8 needles and Yarn C, cast on 3 sts.
Row 1 (RS) K1, P1, K1.
Row 2 Inc in first st, K1, inc in last st. 5 sts.
Row 3 Knit.
Row 4 Inc in first st, knit to last 2 sts, inc in next st, K1. 7 sts.
Cont in broken-rib stitch, inc one st at both ends of every alternate row 15 times while at the same time maintaining the continuity of the pattern. 59 sts.
Bind off 6 sts at beg of next 9 rows. 5 sts.
Bind off remaining stitches.

Section 5

Repeat section 4 using Yarn E.

STRIPED EDGING

Using Size 8 needles and Yarn A, cast on 22 stitches.
The striped edging is worked in broken-rib stitch.
Row 1 K1, * P1, K1; rep from * to end.
Row 2 P1, * K1, P1; rep from * to end.
Rows 3 and 4 Knit.
These 4 rows form the pattern.
Repeat rows 1–4 twice. 12 rows worked in Yarn A in all.
Cut Yarn A.
Join Yarn C.
Repeat rows 1–4 three times. 12 rows worked in Yarn C.
Cut Yarn C.
Join Yarn E.
Repeat rows 1–4 three times. 12 rows worked in Yarn E.
Cut Yarn E.
Three stripes and 36 rows worked in all.
Repeat these 36 rows 9 times. 30 stripes worked in all.
Bind off using Yarn E.

UNDERSIDE (Make 2)

Using Size 8 needles and Yarn F, cast on 66 sts.

Row 1 K2, * P2, K2; rep from * to end.
Row 2 P2, * K2, P2; rep from * to end.
Repeat rows 1 and 2 twice.

Begin basket-stitch pattern.
Row 1 Knit.
Row 2 Purl.
Row 3 K2, *P2, K2; rep from * to end.
Row 4 P2, *K2, P2; rep from * to end.
Rows 1–4 form the pattern.

Work 16 more rows in patt, inc one st at both ends of 4th, 8th, 12th and 16th rows. 74 sts.
Work 8 rows straight in patt.
Work 38 rows patt, dec one 1 st at both ends of first row and every foll alt row. 36 sts.
Bind off 2 at the beg of the next 4 rows. 28 sts.
Bind off 3 at the beg of the next 4 rows. 16 sts.
Bind off 4 at the beg of the next 2 rows. 8 sts.
Bind off remaining stitches.

CENTRAL KNITTED BALL

Using Size 8 needles and two strands of Yarn B, cast on 15 sts.
Row 1 Knit.
Repeating row 1 forms garter stitch.
Work 19 more rows in garter st.
Bind off and cut yarn leaving a long tail.
Thread the tail through a large tapestry needle and work running stitches all around the edge of the square and gather up.
Insert fiberfill inside and sew up to create a knitted ball.

FINISHING

Block each piece following the instructions on page 138 and referring to the yarn label.
Using Yarn B or Yarn D, join the 5 front sections together, creating a circle for the top of the cushion.
Join the cast-on and bound-off ends of the striped edging.
Join the striped edging to the cushion top, 6 edging stripes to each front segment, easing any excess length into the seam.
Overlap the two semicircular pieces for the underside by approximately 7 inches (18cm), with the rib edges toward the center. The overlap forms the opening for the pillow form.
Mattress-stitch (see pages 138–39) or backstitch around the curved outer edges to join the pieces together, forming the circle for the underside.
Join the underside of the cover to the other side of the striped edging.
Sew the knitted ball to the center of the cover top. Insert the pillow form.

Lacy-Knit Runner

Emma Seddon

MATERIALS

Three 1¾oz (50g) balls Be Sweet Bamboo, shade 627 (Yarn A)
One 1¾oz (50g) ball Be Sweet Bamboo, shade 644 (Yarn B)
One 1¾oz (50g) ball Be Sweet Bamboo, shade 645 (Yarn C)
One 1¾oz (50g) ball Be Sweet Bamboo, shade 613 (Yarn D)
One 1¾oz (50g) ball Be Sweet Bamboo, shade 670 (Yarn E)
One 1¾oz (50g) ball Be Sweet Bamboo, shade 640 (Yarn F)
One 1¾oz (50g) ball Be Sweet Bamboo, shade 651 (Yarn G)
One 1¾oz (50g) ball Be Sweet Bamboo, shade 655 (Yarn H)
One 1¾oz (50g) ball Be Sweet Bamboo, shade 652 (Yarn I)
Pair each Size 6 (4mm) and Size 5 (3.75mm) knitting needles
Beads and mother-of-pearl buttons (⅜ inch/1cm diameter) to decorate
Sewing needle and thread

MEASUREMENTS

Width 8¼ inches (21cm)
Length 43½ inches (110cm)
The runner can be made wider by adding extra pattern repeats. For
each pattern repeat cast on an extra 5 stitches. Each pattern repeat
will increase the width by 1 inch (2.5cm) and will need about an extra
½oz (12g)of Yarn A. Add more flowers to fill the extra width.

GAUGE

20 sts and 30 rows = 4 inches (10cm) square measured over pattern using
Yarn A and Size 6 needles or the size required to obtain the correct gauge.

ABBREVIATIONS

See page 129.

RUNNER

Using Size 6 needles and Yarn A, cast on 40 sts.
Row 1 Purl.
Continue in pattern.
Row 1 (RS) * K3, yo, K2tog; rep from * to end.
Rows 2, 4, 6, and 8 Purl.
Row 3 Knit.
Row 5 K3, * K3, yo, K2tog; repeat from * to last 2 sts, K2.
Row 7 Knit.
These 8 rows form the pattern.
Repeat these 8 rows until runner measures 43½ inches (110cm),
ending with a WS row.
Bind off.

made with silky Be Sweet Bamboo yarn, this beautiful lacy-knit runner, scattered with colorful flowers and leaves, looks gorgeous adorning a shelf, mantelpiece, chest of drawers, or dressing table. Make as many or as few of the flowers and leaves as you like. Use up any odds and ends of trimming or buttons or beads that you have, and bring a touch of summer garden into your home.

FINISHING

Block runner following the instructions on page 138 and referring to the yarn label.

Work Antwerp stitch (or blanket stitch) around the edges.

LARGE FRONDS/CURLICUES (Make 3 in Yarn F and 2 in Yarn G)

Using Size 6 needles, cast on 15 sts.

Row 1 (P1, K1, P1) into each st on the row. 45 sts.

Bind off loosely.

SMALL FRONDS (Make 2 in Yarn F and 2 in Yarn G)

Using Size 6 needles, cast on 10 sts.

Row 1 (P1, K1, P1) into each st on the row. 30 sts.

Bind off loosely.

LEAVES (Make 2 in Yarn F and 2 in Yarn G)

Using Size 6 needles, cast on 3 sts.

Row 1 and every alternate row to row 17 Purl.

Row 2 Knit.

Row 4 K1, * M1, K1; repeat from * once. 5 sts.

Row 6 K2, M1, K1, M1, K2. 7 sts.

Row 8 K3, M1, K1, M1, K3. 9 sts.

Row 10 K2, K2tog, yo, K1, yo, K2tog tbl, K2. 9 sts.

Row 12 Repeat row 10. 9 sts.

Row 14 K1, sl1, K2tog, psso, yo, K1, yo, K2tog tbl, pass st just worked back to LHN, pick up 2nd st on LHN and pass over first st and drop off LHN, return st knitted back to RHN, K1. 7 sts.

Row 16 K1, K2tog, K1, K2tog tbl, K1. 5 sts.

Row 18 K1, sl1, K2tog tbl, psso, K1. 3 sts.

Row 19 P3tog. 1 st.

Fasten off.

FRILLY-EDGES FLOWER–PANSY (Color 1–Make 1)

Using Size 6 needles and Yarn D, cast on 48 sts.

Row 1 K1, * K2, slip first st knitted over 2nd st on RHN and drop off; repeat from * to last st, K1. 25 sts.

Cut Yarn D.

Join Yarn B.

Row 2 P1, * P2 tog; repeat from * to end. 13 sts.

Row 3 * K2tog; repeat from * to last st, K1. 7 sts.

Cut yarn, leaving a long tail. Thread the tail through the remaining stitches and pull tightly to create a flower.

Sew in ends and, if necessary, join the seam.

FRILLY-EDGES FLOWER–PANSY (Color 2–Make 1)

Using Size 6 needles and Yarn E, cast on 48 sts.

Cut Yarn E.

Join Yarn I.

Row 1 K1, * K2, slip first st knitted over 2nd st on RHN and drop off; repeat from * to last st, K1. 25 sts.

Cut Yarn I.

Join Yarn C.

Row 2 P1, * P2 tog; repeat from * to end. 13 sts.

Row 3 * K2tog; repeat from * to last st, K1. 7 sts.

Cut yarn, leaving a long tail. Thread the tail through the remaining stitches and pull tightly to create a flower.

Sew in ends and, if necessary, join the seam.

LARGE PICOT KNITTED FLOWER (Make 1 in each of Yarn B, Yarn E, and Yarn H)

Using Size 6 needles, cast on 7 sts.

Row 1 Bind off 6 sts.

Row 2 Cast on 6 sts.

Repeat rows 1 and 2 three times.

Row 9 Bind off 6 sts. (5 picots made)

Join into a circle by inserting RHN into top of first stitch, wrapping the yarn around the needle and drawing up a stitch (2 sts on RHN). Pass the first stitch over the 2nd stitch, then fasten off the remaining stitch.

SMALL PICOT KNITTED FLOWER (Make 2 in Yarn C, 2 in Yarn D, 2 in Yarn H, 1 in Yarn B, and 1 in Yarn E)

Using Size 6 needles, cast on 5 sts.

Row 1 Bind off 4 sts.

Row 2 Cast on 4 sts.

Repeat rows 1 and 2 three times.

Row 9 Bind off 4 sts. (5 picots made)

Complete as for picot knitted flower.

KNITTED FLOWER–DAISY (Color 1–Make 1)

Using Size 6 needles and Yarn B, cast on 57 sts.

Row 1 Purl.

Row 2 K2, * K1, slip this st back onto LHN, pass the next 8 sts on LHN over this stitch and off the LHN, yo2, knit the first st again, K2; repeat from * to end. 27 sts.

Row 3 P1, * P2tog, (P1, P1 tbl) into the yo2 of previous row, P1; rep from * to last st, P1. 22 sts.

Row 4 * K2 tog; repeat from * to end. 11 sts.

Row 5 Purl.

Thread the tail through the remaining stitches and pull tightly to create a flower. Sew in ends and, if necessary, join the seam.

KNITTED FLOWER–DAISY (Color 2–Make 1)

Using Size 6 needles and Yarn C, cast on 57 sts.

Row 1 Purl.

Cut Yarn C.

Join Yarn E.

Complete as for knitted flower–Daisy Color 1, beginning at row 2.

TRUMPET FLOWERS (Make 1 in each of Yarn C, Yarn E, and Yarn D)

These flowers begin with a provisional cast-on.

Using Size 5 needles and a contrasting yarn, cast on 14 sts.

Rows 1 and 2 Knit.

Cut contrasting yarn.

Join main yarn, leaving a long tail

Work 6 rows st-st, beg with a knit row.

Row 9 K1, * yo, K2tog; repeat from * to last st, K1. 14 sts.

Change to Size 6 needles.

Work 5 rows st-st, beg with a purl row.

Next row Unravel the contrasting yarn and put the stitches in the main yarn onto a spare Size 5 needle with the point facing in the same direction as the main needle.

Hold the needles with the stitches parallel, with the WS facing each other. * Using a Size 5 needle, insert the tip of RHN knitwise into the first stitch on the front LHN then knitwise into the first stitch on the back LHN and knit both stitches together and off the LHNs.

Rep from * to end of row. 14 sts.

Next row Purl.

Cut yarn, leaving a long tail. Thread tail through the remaining stitches.

Join the side seam with mattress stitch (see pages 138–39).

Pull the stitches together to create a flower and fasten off.

KNITTED BALL (Make 2 in each of Yarn I and Yarn H)

Using Size 6 needles, cast on 1 st.

Row 1 (K1, P1, K1) into same stitch. 3 sts.

Row 2 P into front and back of first st, P1, P into front and back of 3rd st. 5 sts.

Work 4 rows st-st, beg with a knit row.

Row 7 K2 tog, K1, K2 tog. 3 sts.

Row 8 P3tog.

Fasten off.

To create a knitted ball, use the cast on and bound-off tails to sew onto the main runner fabric as close together as possible to create a 3-D shape.

BERRY (Make 1 in Yarn B and 1 in Yarn D)

These flowers begin with a provisional cast-on.

Using Size 6 needles and a contrasting yarn, cast on 14 sts.

Rows 1 and 2 Knit.

Cut contrasting yarn.

Join main yarn, leaving a long tail.

Row 3 Knit. Thread the end left at the beginning of this row through all 14 sts on the needle, leaving the stitches on the needle.

Work 4 rows st-st, beg with a purl row.

Cut main yarn leaving a long tail. Thread the tail through the stitches on the needle. Remove the contrasting yarn. Pull both tails to gather the stitches then join side seam with mattress stitch. Fasten off.

FINISHING

This pattern has been given as a starting point, but you may prefer to make more of one flower than another, or to substitute beads for the buttons. The colors used, as well as the shape and size of the buttons and/or beads, can vary according to your taste or décor. In addition, each piece, especially the picot knitted flowers and the curlicues, can be varied in length by increasing or decreasing the number of stitches used.

Lay the finished flowers, berries, leaves, beads, and buttons on the base fabric, using the photograph as a guide if you wish. When you are happy with their positioning, pin and sew them in place.

Threading ribbon through the eyelets horizontally or along each end would create a very feminine touch. Increasing the length of the stitching around the main fabric would allow a narrow ribbon to be threaded through the eyelets created.

the ultimate symbol of love and romance, heart-shaped lavender sachets make lovely presents and can be strewn all around the home. Make as many as you like, in lots of different colors, and hang them from ribbons on hooks, prop them up on shelves, lay them on the bed, or place them inside drawers or closets to scent clothes or bed linens. You could even embroider initials on the front in chain stitch or running stitch if you wish.

Lavender Heart   Catherine Tough

MATERIALS
One 3½oz (100g) hank Manos del Uruguay, shade 2190 Raspberry (Yarn A)
One 3½oz (100g) hank Manos del Uruguay, shade 2148 Rose (Yarn B)
Pair Size 6 (5mm) knitting needles
20 inches (50cm) square bright pink jersey fabric
Sewing machine, needle and matching thread
Dried lavender and funnel
8 inches (20cm) pink velvet ribbon, ⅝ inch (15mm) wide for loop

MEASUREMENTS
Width 6¾ inches (17cm)
Length without hanging loop 6¾ inches (17cm)

GAUGE
15 sts = 4 inches (10cm) square measured over stockinette stitch using Size 8 needles or the size required to obtain the correct gauge.
11 sts = 4 inches (10cm) square measured over pattern using Size 8 needles or the size required to obtain the correct gauge.
The correct gauge is not a requirement.

ABBREVIATIONS
See page 129.

FRONT
Using Size 8 needles and Yarn A, make a 9-inch (23cm) square in the following textured stitch:

Cast on 26 sts or the even number of stitches to give the finished width of 9 inches (23cm).
Row 1 (WS) Knit.
Row 2 (RS) K2, * K1 on row below, K1; rep from * to end.
Row 3 Knit.
Row 4 * K1, K1 on row below; rep from * last 2 sts, K2.
Repeating rows 1–4 forms the pattern.
Work in patt until work measures 9 inches (23cm). Bind off.

BACK
Using Size 8 needles and Yarn B, make a 9-inch (23cm) square in stockinette stitch:
Cast on 35 sts or the number of stitches to give the finished width of 9 inches (23cm).
Work in stockinette stitch until work measures 9 inches (23cm). Bind off.

FINISHING
Block each piece following the instructions on page 138 and referring to the yarn labels, or press with a steam iron and leave to dry.
With right sides together, sandwich the knitted squares between two layers of jersey fabric and pin, then draw a heart shape onto the fabric. Fold the ribbon in half and slip the loop between the knitted pieces, in the middle of the heart shape, with the ends upward. Machine-stitch along the heart outline, leaving a 2-inch (5cm) gap on one side. Trim close to the stitching and turn heart right side out. Fill it with lavender and slipstitch up the edges of the opening together.

do as the British do, and keep tea hot with a tea cozy! Like a giant chocolate cupcake in its jaunty pink-and-white striped case, complete with frosting, multicolored sprinkles, and a juicy red cherry on top, this enchanting and whimsical tea cozy will be the focal point of your tea table.

Cupcake Tea Cozy   Donna Wilson with Pauline Hornsby

MATERIALS

Two 1¾oz (50g) balls Rowan Pure Wool DK, shade 028 Raspberry
(Yarn A)

One 1¾oz (50g) ball Rowan Pure Wool DK, shade 013 Enamel (Yarn B)

One 1¾oz (50g) ball Debbie Bliss Baby Cashmerino, shade 11 Brown
(Yarn C)

One 1¾oz (50g) ball Rowan Pure Wool DK, shade 041 Scarlet (Yarn D)

2-ply embroidery thread in pink, brown, red, green, and yellow or
scraps of wool knitting yarn in green and yellow

Pair Size 3 (3.25mm) knitting needles

Pair Size 6 (4mm) knitting needles

Tapestry needle

MEASUREMENTS

Circumference at bottom 18 inches (46cm)

Height (excluding cherry) 8½ inches (22cm)

GAUGE

26 stitches and 34 rows = 4 inches (10cm) square measure over
stockinette stitch using Baby Cashmerino on Size 3 needles or the
size required to give the correct gauge.

22 stitches and 30 rows = 4 inches (10cm) square measured over
stockinette stitch using Pure Wool DK on Size 6 needles or the size
required to give the correct gauge.

26 stitches and 30 rows = 4 inches (10cm) square measured over
striped pattern using Pure Wool DK on Size 6 needles or the size
required to give the correct gauge. When stranding the usual yarn at
the back of the work it alters the gauge. The act of pulling the yarn
behind will tighten the gauge to be the same as for the Baby
Cashmerino yarn (26 sts and 34 rows).

ABBREVIATIONS

See page 129.

NOTES

The tea cozy is made in two identical halves, which are then sewn
together. The pattern starts at the top of the lining and finishes at
the top of the right side of the cozy.

When short-row shaping, refer to the wrapping technique on page 133.

TEA COZY (Make 2)

Using Size 6 needles and Yarn A, cast on 33 sts.

Row 1 (RS of lining) K20, turn.

Row 2 P7, turn.

Row 3 K11, turn.

Row 4 P15, turn.

Row 5 K19, turn.

Row 6 P23, turn.

Row 7 K26, turn.

Row 8 P29, turn.

Row 9 K31, turn.

Row 10 Purl all 33 sts.

Beg with a knit row, work 10 rows st-st, inc 1 st at each end of first
row and foll 4 alt rows, ending with a purl row. 43 sts.

Beg with a knit row, work 28 rows st-st, inc 1 st at each end of first,
3rd, 7th, and 11th rows, ending with a purl row. 51 sts.

Increase for striped pattern.

Next row (RS) [K3, M1, K4, M1] 7 times, K2. 65 sts.

Lining now completed.

Start striped pattern.

Join Yarn B.

Next row (WS) * P1 Yarn A, P1 Yarn B; rep from * to last st, P1 Yarn A.

Next row (RS) K1 Yarn A, *K1 Yarn B, K1 Yarn A; rep from * to end.

These 2 rows form the striped pattern.

Work 12 more rows in striped pattern.

Cut Yarns A and B.

Change to Size 3 needles

Join Yarn C.

Beg with a purl row (WS), work 16 rows st-st.

Join Yarn B but do not cut Yarn C.

Beg with a purl row and Yarn B, work 2 rows st-st.

Cut Yarn B.

Rejoin Yarn C.

Beg with a purl row, work 16 rows st-st, dec 1 st at each end of 6th,
10th, 14th, and 16th rows, thus ending with a knit row. 57 sts.

Cut Yarn C.

Change to Size 6 needles.

Join Yarn B.

Row 1 (WS) [P2, P2tog] 14 times, P1. 43 sts.

Beg with a knit row, work 10 rows st-st, dec 1 st at each end of first row and foll 4 alt rows. 33 sts.

Next row (RS) K31, turn.

Next row P29, turn.

Next row K26, turn.

Next row P23, turn.

Next row P23, turn.

Next row K19, turn.

Next row P15, turn.

Next row K11, turn.

Next row P7, turn.

Next row K20, turn.

Bind off all 33 sts loosely purlwise.

CHERRY

Using Size 3 needles and either Yarn A or Yarn B, cast on 7 sts.

Work 2 rows in garter st.

Cut yarn.

Join Yarn D.

Row 1 Knit, leaving a long tail. Thread the tail left at the beginning of this row through all 7 sts on the needle, leaving the stitches on the needle.

Row 2 (RS) [K1 then K1 tbl into same stitch] 6 times, K1. 13 sts.

Row 3 Purl.

Row 4 * K1, [K1 then K1 tbl into same stitch]; rep from * 5 times, K1. 19 sts.

Row 5 Purl.

Row 6 [K1, K2tog] 6 times, K1. 13 sts.

Row 7 Purl.

Row 8 [K2tog] 6 times, K1. 7 sts.

Cut Yarn D.

Thread Yarn D through all 7 sts on the needle. Pull firmly to gather and close, then use the same thread to join the side seam.

Wind Yarn D around first and second fingers of left hand and use the resulting loop to stuff the cherry.

Remove Yarn A or Yarn B at cast-on. Pull the cast-on tail through all the stitches on the first row of Yarn D to gather and close, adjusting stuffing as necessary. Secure thread and leave the tail for sewing on the cherry.

FINISHING

Block both halves of the cozy following the instructions on page 138 and referring to the yarn labels.

PM at side edges between the 14th and 15th rows of the lining, counting the 20 sts of the first row after the cast-on as the first row.

PM at side edges between the 14th and 15th rows before the bind-off, counting the 20 sts of the last row before the bind-off as the first row.

PM at side edges between the 9th and 10th rows of the lining, counting the last row of the lining before the striped pattern as the first row.

PM at side edges between the 8th and 9th row of the striped pattern, counting the first row of the striped pattern after the lining as the first row.

Place both halves of the tea cozy together, wrong sides facing, lining opposite lining and outer opposite outer.

Join the top (white) section of the outer cozy with mattress stitch between the markers (see page 138-39). (Between 14th and 15th rows on one side edge, the bound-off stitches, and then between 14th and 15th rows on opposite side edge.)

Using 2-ply embroidery thread, embroider straight stitches over the top white section of the outer to resemble sugar sprinkles. If preferred, cut lengths of Yarns A, C, D, and scraps of green and yellow knitting yarns, split into their component threads. Use two threads of the same color to embroider.

Join the top section of the lining with mattress stitch between the markers. (Between 14th and 15th rows on one side edge, the bound-off stitches, and then between 14th and 15th rows on opposite side edge.)

Join the middle side sections of the cozy with mattress stitch between the markers, lining to lining and outer to outer.

Sew in as many ends as possible at this stage.

Push the lining into the outer of the cozy.

Join the four seams of the lining to the outer with mattress stitch, thus leaving holes for the handle and spout.

Attach the cherry to the center top of the outer, passing the sewing thread through the center top of the lining as well as the outer to keep it in position.

Techniques

Abbreviations

alt	alternate (every other)
cm	centimeter(s)
CN	cable needle
col	color
beg	begin(ning)
dec	decrease
foll	follow(s)(ing)
g	grams
inc	increase(ing)
inc 1	increase one stitch by working into the front and back of the next stitch
K	knit
K2tog	knit two stitches together
LHN	left-hand needle
M1	make one stitch by picking up the strand between the needles and working into the back of it
mm	millimeters
oz	ounces
P	purl
P2tog	purl two stitches together
patt	pattern
PM	place marker
psso	pass slipped stitch over
p2sso	pass two slipped stitches over
rem	remain(ing)
rep	repeat
rev	reverse
RHN	right-hand needle
rnd	round
RS	right side (of work)
skpo	slip one stitch, knit one stitch, pass slipped stitch over
s2kpo	slip two stitches, knit one stitch, pass two slipped stitches over

sl	slip
sl1K	slip one stitch knitwise
sl1P	slip one stitch purlwise
sl1wyib	slip one stitch with yarn at back of work
sl1wyif	slip one stitch with yarn at/in front of work
sl2wyib	slip two stitches with yarn at back of work
sl2wyif	slip two stitches with yarn at/in front of work
ssk	slip, slip, knit
SM	slip marker
ssp	slip, slip, purl
st-st	stockinette stitch (knit on RS rows, purl on WS rows)
st(s)	(stitch)es
tbl	through back of loop(s)
tog	together
WS	wrong side (of work)
yb	yarn back, take yarn to back of work
yf	yarn forward; bring yarn to front of work
yo	yarn over needle or yarn around needle to make a stitch
yo2	yarn over needle or yarn round needle twice to make two stitches

Special abbreviations for individual patterns are included with the pattern.

Charts

Charts give a visual representation of a piece of knitting when completed and also contain the instructions to complete the knitting. Charts can show a complete piece of knitting such as a sleeve, a color motif, or a stitch pattern such as lace or cable.

Charts are made up of squares, where each square represents a stitch. Up the sides of the chart the rows are numbered from 1, at the bottom right, upward to the last row. Along the bottom of the chart the stitches are numbered from 1, at the bottom right, leftward to the last stitch.

Charts are read from the bottom row upward. Right-side rows are read from right to left and wrong-side rows are read from left to right. Wrong-side rows on the chart show how the knitted fabric will look on the right side.

For multicolor knitting, each of the squares contains the color for that stitch or contains a symbol representing the color for that stitch. For stitch patterns, such as lace or cable, each of the squares contains a symbol for that stitch. Squares for stitches that are knit on right-side rows and purl on wrong-side rows (stockinette stitch) are often left blank. For both multicolor knitting and stitch patterns, a key explains what the symbols mean.

Cast-on

There are many ways to cast on, some using only one needle and some using both, with the stitches cast onto either the right-hand or the left-hand needle. Each method has advantages and disadvantages, and every knitter has a preferred method. However, some cast-on methods suit the following stitch pattern, the final uses of the cast-on, such as for picking up stitches, or the wear and tear of the cast-on better than others. Some methods form a decorative edge by themselves.

GERMAN LONG-TAIL CAST-ON (SEE RIGHT)

Also known as the Continental cast-on, this method uses one needle and two strands of yarn. It produces a strong and elastic edge.

1 Place the slip loop on the right-hand needle to make the first stitch. When making the slip loop, leave a tail at least three times the width to be cast on.
2 Hold the ball end and tail yarns in the left hand.
3 Wrap the tail end around the left thumb by moving the thumb clockwise.
4 Lift the ball end with the left forefinger.
5 Insert the tip of the right-hand needle into the strand at the front of the thumb and then insert the needle from top to bottom through the strand on the forefinger.
6 Bring the strand on the forefinger through the strand on the thumb to make a stitch on the right-hand needle.
7 Tighten the strands.
8 Repeat from step 3.

BACKWARD LOOP CAST-ON (SEE FAR RIGHT)

Also known as the Provincial cast-on, twisted loop cast-on, or single thumb cast-on, this method uses one needle and a single strand of yarn. It produces a soft edge.

1 Place the slip loop onto the right-hand needle to make the first stitch.

GERMAN LONG-TAIL CAST-ON

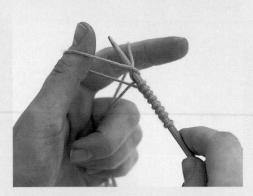

2 Close all four fingers of the left hand over the ball end of the yarn, with the end attached to the needle held between the thumb and the left forefinger.
3 Move the thumb from left to right under the needle end of the yarn and wrap the end around the left thumb by moving the thumb clockwise.
4 Insert the tip of the right-hand needle from

BACKWARD LOOP CAST-ON

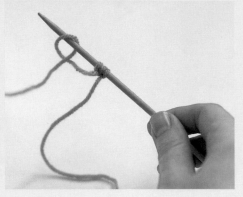

bottom to top into the strand at the front of the thumb and transfer the loop to the needle.
5 Tighten the loop to form the stitch.
6 Repeat from step 3.

CABLE CAST-ON (SEE OPPOSITE)

This cast-on method uses two needles and a single strand of yarn. It produces a strong and elastic edge.

1 Place the slip loop on the left-hand needle to make the first stitch.
2 (a) Insert the right-hand needle into the stitch. Wrap the yarn around the tip of the right-hand needle and draw the yarn through to form a loop. OR
(b) Insert the right-hand needle under the left-hand needle to the left of the slip loop. Wrap the yarn around the tip of the right-hand needle and draw it through.
3 Place the loop just made on the left-hand needle to make the next stitch.
4 Insert the right-hand needle between the first two stitches on the left-hand needle. Wrap the yarn around the tip of the right-hand needle and draw the yarn through to form a loop.
5 Place the loop just made on the left-hand needle to make the next stitch.
6 Repeat steps 4 and 5.

CABLE CAST-ON

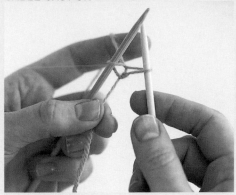

Bind-off

STANDARD OR CHAIN BIND-OFF

Binding off is usually performed knitwise (knitting each stitch before binding it off). Sometimes the stitches are bound off purlwise or in pattern (working the stitch pattern at the same time as binding off the stitches). The pattern will state the method to use.

1 Knit the first two stitches.

2 Insert the tip of the left-hand needle into the second stitch on the right-hand needle (the first stitch that was knitted) and lift it over the first stitch on the right-hand needle (the second stitch that was knitted) and off the needle. One stitch has been bound off.

3 Knit the next stitch.

4 Insert the tip of the left-hand needle into the second stitch on the right-hand needle and lift it over the first stitch on the right-hand needle and off the needle.

5 Repeat steps 3 and 4.

6 When binding off all the stitches, when the end of the row is reached, cut the yarn and thread it through the last stitch. Pull the yarn to close the stitch.

7 When binding off at the beginning of a row, after the required number of stitches has been bound off there will be one stitch remaining on the right-hand needle. Complete the remainder of the row as stated in the pattern.

THREE NEEDLE BIND-OFF

A variation of the standard bind-off, this joins two pieces of knitting together with one bind-off. It produces a neat seam, which is often used at shoulders. When each knitted piece is complete, do not bind off; leave the stitches on a spare needle or a holder.

1 For binding off, the stitches of each piece should be on a needle the same size as that used for the knitting.

2 Place the two pieces right sides together with the stitches at the top and the points of the needles facing in the same direction.

3 Insert the third (empty) right-hand needle knitwise into the first stitch of the front piece and then knitwise into the first stitch of the back piece and knit them together, slipping both stitches off left-hand needles. One stitch on the right-hand needle.

4 Repeat step 3 for the next stitch from each piece. Two stitches on the right-hand needle.

5 Insert the tip of the left-hand needle into

the second stitch on the right-hand needle and lift it over the first stitch on the right-hand needle and off the needle. One stitch on the right-hand needle.

6 Repeat steps 4 and 5.

7 When all the stitches are bound off, at the end of the row cut the yarn and thread it through the last stitch on the right-hand needle. Pull the yarn to close the stitch.

THREE NEEDLE BIND-OFF

Gauge

Make the swatch! Make the swatch! Make the swatch! This cannot be emphasized enough. A slight difference in gauge for unfitted items such as wraps, throws, and toys can fall within acceptable tolerances, but for everything else a gauge swatch is essential. Just think of how much time and money you will spend making a beautiful garment, only to find that it is too tight or hangs so loosely it looks dreadful. Making a gauge swatch is worth every minute of the half hour or so it takes to knit.

MAKING A GAUGE SWATCH

1 Find out from the pattern the number of stitches and rows to 4 inches (10cm) over the stitch pattern.
2 Using the needle size stated in the pattern, cast on the number of stitches to make a swatch 6–8 inches (15–20cm) wide in the stitch pattern.
3 Work the number of rows necessary to make the swatch 6–8 inches (15–20cm). Bind off.
4 Block the swatch (see page 138).
5 Pin the swatch to a towel or flat pad, without stretching.
6 Lay a ruler or tape measure across a straight horizontal row of stitches in the middle of the swatch. Place a pin an inch or two from one edge, then place a pin 4 inches (10cm) farther on.
7 Count the stitches between the pins.
8 Then lay the ruler or tape measure along a straight vertical line of stitches in the middle of the swatch. Insert pins, measuring off 4 inches (10cm) as before.
9 Count the number of rows between the pins.
10 If there are more stitches or rows to 4 inches (10cm) than stated in the pattern, your knitting is too tight. Try again using thicker needles.
11 If there are fewer stitches or rows to 4 inches (10cm) than stated in the pattern, your knitting is too loose. Try again using thinner needles.

Increases

Increases make an extra stitch. They are used when shaping a piece of knitted fabric or for keeping the knitted fabric the same width when starting a stitch pattern that draws in or narrows the knitting, such as cables.

INCREASE 1 OR WORKING INTO THE FRONT AND BACK OF A STITCH

This is a simple method of increasing, but leaves a visible "bar" at the increase. The "bar" is formed after the main stitch, so if increasing at both ends of a row, one fewer stitch is worked before the increase at the end of the row than at the beginning of the row in order to keep the number of stitches between the side edge and the "bar" the same. For example, if three stitches are worked before the stitch with the increase at the beginning of the row, four stitches will be worked after the increase at the end of the row.

This type of increase is often written as "inc 1" to distinguish it from other types of increases.

1 Knit or purl the stitch according to the stitch pattern, but do not slip the stitch off the needle.
2 Knit or purl the stitch again through the back of the stitch, and slip the stitch just knitted off the left-hand needle.

RAISED INCREASE

This is another simple method of increasing. The increases are made between the stitches so that it is easy to keep the number of stitches between the side edge and the increases consistent.

This type of increase is often written as "M1" to distinguish it from other types of increases.

1 For an increase on the right-hand side of the knitted fabric, insert the left-hand needle from front to back into the strand between the needles and knit or purl into the back of

it according to the stitch pattern. The strand will twist when worked to prevent a hole.
2 For an increase on the left-hand side of the knitted fabric, insert the left-hand needle from back to front into the strand between the needles and knit or purl into it according to the stitch pattern. When the left-hand needle is turned to the working position, the strand will twist and, when knitted or purled, will prevent a hole.

Decreases

Decreases remove a stitch. They are used when shaping a piece of knitted fabric or for keeping the knitted fabric the same width when starting a stitch pattern that widens the knitting, such as some lace patterns, or when finishing a stitch pattern that draws in or narrows the knitting, such as cables. When shaping, as for raglans, decreases are worked as paired decreases, where the decreases in each side are mirror images of each other.

KNIT TWO STITCHES TOGETHER

This decrease slopes to the right and is written as "K2tog."

1 Insert the right-hand needle knitwise into the second stitch on the left-hand needle and then knitwise into the first stitch on the left-hand needle.
2 Work a knit stitch through both stitches on the left-hand needle at the same time.

PURL TWO STITCHES TOGETHER

This decrease is used on a purl or wrong-side row where knitting two stitches together would be used on a knit or right-side row. This decrease is written as "P2tog."

1 Insert the right-hand needle purlwise into the first stitch on the left-hand needle and then purlwise into the second stitch on the left-hand needle.
2 Work a purl stitch through both stitches on the left-hand needle at the same time.

SLIP, SLIP, KNIT

This decrease slopes to the left and is written as "ssk."

1 Slip the first stitch and the second stitch knitwise one at a time from the left-hand needle onto the right-hand needle.
2 Insert the left-hand needle from back to front into these two stitches, with the tip of the left-hand needle in front of the tip of the right-hand needle.
3 Work a knit stitch through both stitches at the same time.

SLIP, SLIP, PURL

This decrease is used on a purl or wrong-side row where slip, slip, knit would be used on a knit or right-side row. This decrease is written as "ssp."

1 Slip the first stitch and the second stitch knitwise one at a time from the left-hand needle onto the right-hand needle.
2 Return both stitches one at a time to the left-hand needle without twisting them.
3 Insert the right-hand needle purlwise into the second stitch on the left-hand needle and then purlwise into the first stitch on the left-hand needle.
3 Work a purl stitch through both stitches on the left-hand needle at the same time.

Short rows

"Short rows" is the term for when knitting is turned before the end of the row and the stitches that were then only on the right-hand needle are worked on the next row. This results in more rows being worked on one part of the knitted fabric than on the other. The number of stitches before the turn does not have to be the same every time. Short rows are used for shaping—for example, for shoulders, collars, or the heel of a sock.

When the knitting is turned in the middle of the row, a hole appears. This can be avoided by a technique known as "wrapping" or the "invisible" turn.

TURNING ON KNIT ROWS

1 Work to the position of the turn.
2 Bring the yarn forward between the needles.
3 Slip the next stitch purlwise.
4 Take the yarn back between the needles.
5 Return the slipped stitch to the left-hand needle.
6 Turn the work. The yarn is now in the correct position for purling back, and the slipped stitch is now "wrapped."
7 When working the turn on a subsequent row, work the wrap together with the slipped stitch for an "invisible" turn.

TURNING ON PURL ROWS

1 Work to the position of the turn.
2 Take the yarn back between the needles.
3 Slip the next stitch purlwise.
4 Bring the yarn forward between the needles.
5 Return the slipped stitch to the left-hand needle.
6 Turn the work. The yarn is now in the correct position for knitting back, and the slipped stitch is now "wrapped."
7 When working the turn on a subsequent row, work the wrap together with the slipped stitch for an "invisible" turn.

Cables

Cables are much easier to work than they look. Cables are groups of stitches that cross over each other; where the stitches switch places within a row, they make a twist.

Simple cables are worked as columns of stockinette stitch, with the cables or twists at regular intervals. Cables are usually worked on a background of reverse stockinette stitch, which gives them a raised or three-dimensional effect. The crossing over of the stitches pulls in the knitted fabric, and more stitches are needed than the equivalent width worked in stockinette stitch.

The crossing over of the stitches is worked with a cable needle. This is a short knitting needle with points at both ends. It may have a wide V shape in the middle, or it may be hook shaped. The cable needle should not be thicker than the needles used for the main knitting.

The instructions for cable are written as "CXB" or "CXF," where CX refers to the number of stitches to cable and B or F means to cable these stitches to the back or the front. CXB twist to the right and CXF twist to the left.

CABLE STITCHES (BACK)

1 Slip half the number of stitches stated in CXB onto the cable needle (for example, for C6B slip three stitches onto the cable needle) and hold the cable needle at the back of the work.
2 Knit the remaining half of the number of stitches stated in CXB from the left-hand needle.
3 Knit all the stitches from the cable needle.

CABLE STITCHES (BACK)

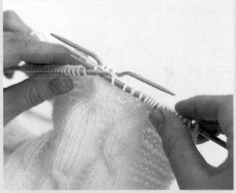

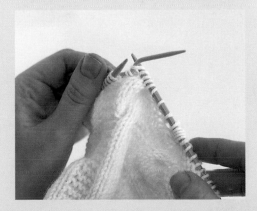

CABLE STITCHES (FRONT)

1 Slip half the number of stitches stated in CXF onto the cable needle (for example, for C6F slip three stitches onto the cable needle) and hold the cable needle at the front of the work.

2 Knit the remaining half of the number of stitches stated in CXF from the left-hand needle.

3 Knit all the stitches from the cable needle.

Instructions for the cables for the Hot-Water Bottle Cover (pages 90-91) and the Cable Wrap (pages 92-95) are given with those patterns.

CABLE STITCHES (FRONT)

Bobbles

Bobbles are decorative and can be positioned in many ways—for example, rows, columns, diamonds, lattices, or clusters. They can be made in the same or a different color or yarn from the main knitted fabric and in the same or a different stitch, such as stockinette-stitch bobbles on a reverse-stockinette-stitch background.

There are many ways of making knitted-in bobbles—some methods making small bobbles and others making large ones. The basic principle is the same: increasing into a single stitch and then decreasing the stitches that have been made to form a bobble on the right side of the knitted fabric, with one or more rows, or perhaps no rows, worked only on the increased stitches before the decreasing.

Bobbles made by decreasing the stitches with no rows between the increased stitches are also known as knots—particularly if only one or a few stitches are increased. Knitting the increased stitches at the same time as the main knitted fabric before decreasing produces a softer bobble.

The increases can be worked by knitting and purling alternately into the same stitch, by knitting into the front and the back of the stitch alternately, or by working a yarn-over between knit stitches. The decreases can be worked by knitting or purling all the stitches together, or slipping some of the stitches, knitting or purling the remaining stitches together, and then passing the slipped stitches over.

Bobbles can also be added after knitting. Each bobble is made individually and then sewn on.

Bobbles take up more yarn than the equivalent area of stockinette stitch.

BOBBLES

Pressing bobbles will flatten them, so be careful when blocking.

Patterns always give the instructions for making the type of bobble(s) for that pattern.

Bead knitting

Adding beads to knitting adds instant glamour and is easier to do than it looks. Beads can be sewn on after knitting, but this is laborious, and the thread could work loose. Thread all the beads you plan to use onto the yarn before starting to knit. If different types or colors of beads are to be used, make sure they are threaded in the correct order.

BEAD KNITTING

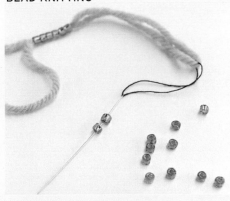

1 Thread a length of sewing thread through the eye of a sewing or beading needle and knot the ends to make a loop; or fold the thread in half to make a loop and thread both cut ends through the needle.
2 Insert the end of the yarn through the loop.
3 Using the needle, thread the beads over the sewing thread and onto the yarn.

POSITIONING A BEAD WITH SLIP STITCH (ON A RIGHT-SIDE ROW)
When knitted in, the beads lie horizontally.

1 Hold the yarn at the front of the work, bringing the yarn forward between the needles if necessary.
2 Push the bead as close as possible to the right-hand needle.
3 Slip the next stitch purlwise so that the bead is positioned in front of this stitch.
4 Continue the row, taking the yarn back between the needles if necessary.

Buttonholes

There are several ways to make a buttonhole, the chosen method being determined partly by the size of the button and by the amount of wear and tear the buttonhole will have. Buttonholes should be large enough to allow the button to pass through, but not so large that the button keeps coming undone.

Patterns give instructions for the position of buttonholes and usually how to make the buttonholes for that pattern.

HORIZONTAL BUTTONHOLE
The horizontal buttonhole is worked over two rows. On the first row, stitches are bound off at the position of the buttonhole, and on the second row the same number of stitches are cast on over the bound-off stitches.

VERTICAL BUTTONHOLE
The vertical buttonhole is worked in two parts. The first row is worked to the position of the buttonhole. Instead of working to the end of the row, the work is turned at this point and these stitches only are worked for the length of the buttonhole. The stitches on the other side of the buttonhole are then worked for the same number of rows. On the next row all the stitches are worked and knitting continues over all stitches.

EYELET BUTTONHOLE
The eyelet buttonhole is suitable for small buttons and is used mainly on babies' and children's garments. It is worked over one row as "yarn over, work two stitches together" or "work two stitches together, yarn over." Working two stitches together (a decrease) next to the yarn-over (an increase) keeps the stitch count correct. A larger eyelet buttonhole can be made by wrapping the yarn twice around the needle instead of once at the yarn-over and dropping the extra loop—to make a larger hole—on the next row.

EYELET BUTTONHOLE

Eyelets

Eyelets are individual holes in knitted fabric, which can be worked as a row or worked into a pattern over several rows, usually on the right side of a stockinette-stitch, reverse-stockinette-stitch, or garter-stitch background. They are characterized by their "yarn over, work two stitches together" type stitch pattern. As in the eyelet buttonhole, the yarn-over increase is compensated for by the "work-two-stitches-together" decreases to maintain the stitch count.

A line of eyelets–horizontal, vertical, or diagonal–makes holes in which to insert a ribbon, cord or elastic (but never around the necks of babies' or children's garments). The eyelets can be spaced close together, far apart, or in a close-far pattern. The background may be rib or another stitch pattern, but preferably not one that is likely to become muddled with the eyelets.

Working eyelets as "yarn over, knit two stitches together"–the increase first–gives a bias to the right. Working eyelets as "knit two stitches together, yarn over"–the increase last–gives a bias to the left. "Slip, slip, knit" or equivalent decreases can be worked instead of "knit two stitches together."

EYELETS

Ways to embellish

I-CORD (KNITTED CORD)

I-cords are circular cords knitted on two double-pointed needles. The result is similar to the cords obtained with French knitting or bobbin knitting. Advantages of knitting I-cords on two needles include using any yarn on any size needles to suit your project, choosing the thickness of the I-cord by having from two to seven stitches (depending on yarn and/or needle thickness), and accurate measurement of length.

Among other uses, I-cords can be used as ties in place of ribbon, for sewing onto knitted or other fabric to make frog fastenings or raised designs, or for hanging pompoms, tassels, or mobiles.

MAKING AN I-CORD

1 Using two double-pointed needles cast on between two and seven stitches.
2 Knit these stitches from the left-hand needle to the right-hand needle.
3 Without turning the needle, push the stitches to the other end of the right-hand needle.
4 Without turning the needle, transfer the needle to the left hand and hold the needle ready to knit the stitches again. The yarn will be hanging at the left of the stitches.
5 Bring the yarn behind the stitches and knit the stitches from the left-hand needle to the right-hand needle.
6 Repeat steps 3–5.
7 To finish, either bind off or cut the yarn, thread the yarn through the stitches, and pull to gather.
8 Sew in the ends.

Commercial French-knitting bobbins are widely available, usually with four prongs, but some are available with a greater number of prongs. If using a commercial bobbin, follow the instructions provided.

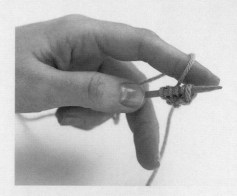

FRINGE

Fringe is often used at the end of scarves and on the edges of shawls. Tassels should be attractively spaced and even in length. You can make fringe as thin or thick as you like by varying the number of strands.

MAKING A SIMPLE FRINGE

1 Cut the yarn into pieces about two-and-a-half times the length of each tassel. Do this by wrapping the yarn around a suitable-sized book and then cutting at one or both ends.
2 With the right side of the knitted fabric facing, insert a crochet hook from back to front at the position of the tassel.
3 Take a group of strands half the thickness of the tassel. Fold the stands in half and wrap the folded end around the crochet hook.
4 Pull the hook from front to back, taking the folded end of the group of strands with it through the knitted fabric to make a loop.

MAKING FRINGE

5 Thread the cut ends of the strands through the loop and pull gently to secure the knot.
6 When all the tassels have been made, make sure they are even and then trim the ends to the same length.

POMPOMS

Pompoms make simple decorative features to use on the top of hats, on the back of gloves, at the end of cords, or wherever you like.

Commercial pompom-making kits are available with templates in three or four sizes. If using one of these kits, follow the instructions provided.

MAKING A POMPOM

1 On a piece of cardboard or plastic, draw a circle with the diameter of the pompom you wish to make. Either use a compass or draw around a circular object, such as a cup.

MAKING A POMPOM

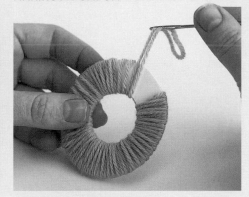

2 In the center of the circle, draw a smaller circle with a diameter one-third to one-half the diameter of the larger circle. The thicker the yarn, the larger the inner circle needs to be.
3 Cut around the outline of the larger circle, then cut out the inner circle.
4 Make another piece in the same way, and place the two circles together.
5 Thread a tapestry needle with your chosen yarn. Take the needle around and around the ring, adding new lengths of yarn as required.
6 When the ring is completely covered with yarn and the hole filled, use sharp scissors to cut the yarn at the outer edge of the circles.
7 Gently pull the two circles away from each other so as not to disturb the cut strands.
8 Wind another length of yarn between the circles, around the center core of the strands, and knot firmly. If sewing on the pompom, leave the ends of this thread uncut.
9 Remove the two cardboard or plastic circles.
10 Fluff out the pompom and trim stray ends.

EMBROIDERY

Embroidery is best worked after blocking and with a yarn that is not so thick as to distort the knitted fabric. Do not work the embroidery stitches too tightly and block the knitted fabric again after embroidering.

FRENCH KNOTS

1 With the right side of the knitted fabric facing, bring the sewing needle, threaded with the yarn for the knot, through from back to front at the position of the knot.
2 Wrap the yarn once or twice around the tip of the needle, then place the needle tip close to where it emerged, holding the yarn with your free hand to keep the loop(s) in place.
3 Take the needle to the back of the work, pulling the thread through the loop(s) quickly and smoothly; fasten on the wrong side.

FRENCH KNOTS

CHAIN STITCH

CHAIN STITCH

When worked in a circle with the bottom of the stitches all starting in the center, this stitch suggests the petals of a flower and is called lazy-diasy stitch.

1 With the right side of the fabric facing, bring the threaded tapestry needle through from back to front at the position of the bottom of the first stitch.
2 Form the yarn into a loop; insert the needle from front to back where it first emerged.
3 Bring the needle up through the fabric again, from back to front, inside the loop at the top of the stitch.
4 Pull the yarn through, but not too tightly, so that the loop is gently rounded and the knitted fabric remains flexible.
5 Take the needle down again inside the loop, where it emerged in step 3, forming a new loop.
6 Repeat steps 3–5.

Weaving in ends

There is no one correct way to weave in ends, but they should be woven in neatly and not seen on the right side of the knitted fabric, leave no holes, have no knots, and, in multicolor knitting, be woven into their own color. When possible, join new balls of yarn at the beginning of a row, but not if that edge is a free edge (not taken into a seam). The ends can be sewn into the edge of the

knitted stitches inside the seam, sewing one end upward and one end downward.

Leave a long end for weaving in, and make sure the end is secure before cutting it, especially with yarns that easily fray or unravel.

When joining yarn in the middle of a row, such as for multicolor knitting, the ends should be sewn in before blocking. Using a sharp sewing needle will split the stitches in the wrong side and help make the weaving in less visible on the right side. Close holes or complete stitches by sewing the end through the adjacent stitch to complete the stitch as if it had been knitted. Ends can also be woven in by following the interlocking lattice of the knitted stitches on the wrong side.

Blocking

Blocking is pinning out a piece of knitted fabric to the correct size and shape, then pressing or damp finishing before sewing up. Blocking gives a smooth finish and proper shape to the knitted fabric, stretching edges that are pulling, sharpening points and corners, and drawing buttonhole slits together. Knitted pieces should be blocked before sewing up, and all mid-row ends should be woven in.

Blocking is done on a blocking pad laid on a firm, flat surface, such as an ironing board, kitchen table, or floor. The blocking pad should be well padded—an old blanket covered with a white cloth or a large folded clean towel will suffice. Pins should be rustless and with glass or other highly visible heads. Err on the side of generosity when using pins.

Read the yarn label to check the pressing instructions. If using more than one yarn, follow the gentlest method of pressing or use the damp-finishing method. Do not press rib, raised patterns, or stitch patterns that would be flattened. Damp finishing is recommended for the novice or the nervous.

PINNING OUT

With the wrong side of the knitting uppermost, pin out each piece to size and shape along the edges, making sure that the rows and the columns of stitches are straight. The pins should be at right angles to the knitting, from the outer edge inward. Do not pin out ribs (unless told to do so), and let the knitting narrow naturally toward ribbed areas.

PRESSING

1 Cover the knitted piece with a white cloth. As a general rule, use a dry cloth for synthetics and a damp cloth for natural fibers, both with a dry iron. Be guided by the pressing instructions on the yarn label.
2 Heat the iron to the correct temperature, as stated on the yarn label.
3 Put the iron on the cloth and immediately lift it up again. Repeat all over the knitted piece. Never use an ironing motion.
4 Leave the cloth in place until cool and/or dry.

DAMP FINISHING

1 Fill a spray bottle with cold water and lightly spray the knitted piece until damp, avoiding ribs.
2 Cover with a clean white cloth and pat gently to absorb excess water.
3 Remove the cloth and allow the knitted piece to dry naturally.

Sewing up

MATTRESS STITCH

Joining knitted pieces using mattress stitch, also known as ladder stitch or the invisible seam, gives a neat seam and can be used to join most knitting stitches, including stockinette stitch, reverse-stockinette stitch, and rib. Sewing is done on the right side of the knitted fabric, making it easier to match shapings, pattern repeats, and stripes. A full stitch is usually taken into the seam, but half a stitch can be taken in for thick yarns. When joining seams with the same number of rows or stitches on each side, it is not necessary to pin the pieces together.

1 Place the pieces to be joined side by side with the right side uppermost.

2 Start at the bottom (cast-on) edge. Bring the threaded sewing needle from the cast-on corner of the right-hand piece, insert from back to front between the first and second cast-on stitches of the left-hand piece, then from back to front between the first and second cast-on stitches of the right-hand piece, and then back again from back to front between the first and second cast-on stitches of the left-hand piece. This makes a figure eight and neatly closes the start of the seam.

3 Between each stitch is a "bar" made by the yarn. Pick up the bar between the first and second stitch on the first row of the right-hand piece.

4 Pick up the bar between the first and second stitch on the first row of the left-hand piece.

5 On the right-hand piece, insert the needle where it came out and pick up the next bar.

MATTRESS STITCH

6 On the left-hand piece, insert the needle where it came out and pick up the next bar.

7 Repeat steps 5 and 6. Every inch or so, pull the sewing yarn firmly to close the seam.

Bound-off and cast-on edges can be joined by taking in one stitch or a half stitch into the seam instead of the "bar." If the yarn is not pulled too tightly, the seaming forms a row of knit stitches.

GRAFTING STOCKINETTE STITCH

Mattress stitch can also be used for joining a cast-on or bound-off edge to a side edge, or when gathering a longer edge to fit a shorter one. Pinning the pieces together will help to keep them evenly matched. Where necessary, pick up two or more bars or stitches instead of one.

KITCHENER STITCH/GRAFTING

This joins two sets of stitches that have not been bound-off, so that the join looks like continuous knitting. Stitches from a provisional cast-on can also be grafted. Stitches not bound off or provisional cast-on stitches can also be grafted to a bound-off edge, a cast-on edge, or a side edge. For the following methods, both needles have the tips pointing to the right.

GRAFTING STOCKINETTE STITCH (SEE LEFT)

1 Lay the knitted pieces knit side up on a flat surface, needle to needle, needles horizontal. Remove some or all stitches from the needles.

2 Thread a tapestry needle with an end-of-row tail from one of the knitted pieces or a new length of yarn (contrast yarn shown here).

3 Working from right to left, insert the tapestry needle from back to front through the first stitch from the bottom needle.

4 Insert the tapestry needle from front to back through the first stitch from the top needle.

5 Insert the tapestry needle from back to front through the next stitch from the top needle.

6 Insert the tapestry needle from front to back through the first stitch from the bottom needle.

7 Insert the tapestry needle from back to front through the next stitch from the bottom needle. One stitch completed. Adjust the tension of the stitch to match the knitting.

8 Repeat steps 4–7.

GRAFTING FROM TWO NEEDLES

1 Hold the needles together with the purl sides of the knitted pieces facing each other.

2 Thread a tapestry needle with an end-of-row tail from one of the knitted pieces or a new length of yarn.

3 Working from right to left, insert the

tapestry needle from back to front through the first stitch on the front needle. Pull the yarn through and leave the stitch on the needle.

4 Insert the tapestry needle from front to back through the first stitch on the back needle. Pull the yarn through and leave the stitch on the needle.

5 Insert the tapestry needle from front to back through the first stitch on the front needle and slip the stitch off the needle.

6 Insert the tapestry needle from back to front into the next stitch on the front needle and leave the stitch on the needle.

7 Insert the tapestry needle from back to front into the first stitch on the back needle and slip the stitch off the needle.

8 Insert the tapestry needle from front to back into the next stitch on the back needle and leave the stitch on the needle.

9 Repeat steps 5 to 8.

DUPLICATE STITCH

This mimics stockinette stitch and is often used to work a small area of color, such as letters, numbers, or a motif. The tapestry needle is inserted in the spaces between the stitches, not into the yarn. The embroidery yarn should be compatible with the knitted fabric and of a thickness to cover the knitted stitch.

1 Hold the fabric with the knit side uppermost; thread a tapestry needle with embroidery yarn.

2 Insert the needle from back to front through the center of the stitch below the stitch to be covered. This is the center bottom of the stitch to be covered.

3 Following the path of the stitch, insert the needle from front to back at the top right or top left of the stitch—top right if you are working from right to left and vice versa.

4 Take the needle behind the stitch and then bring it through from back to front.

5 Insert the needle from front to back into the place where it started. The needle and yarn have traced the path of the stitch to be covered.

6 Repeat steps 2-5.

Suppliers

Loop
41 Cross Street, Islington,
London N1 2BB, U.K.
Tel: +44 (0)20 7288 1160
www.loop.gb.com
All of the yarns and notions shown in this book are available at Loop and Loop's online shop.

Contact the following suppliers or check their websites for information.

YARN
Alchemy Yarns
PO Box 1080, Sebastopol, CA 95473, U.S.A.
Tel: 707 823 3276
www.alchemyyarns.com

Be Sweet
1315 Bridgeway, Sausalito, CA 94965, U.S.A.
Tel: 415 331 9676
www.besweetproducts.com

Blue Sky Alpacas
PO Box 88, Cedar, MN 55011, U.S.A.
Tel: 888 460 8862
www.blueskyalpacas.com

Colinette
Banwy Workshops, Llanfair Caereinion,
Powys, Wales SW21 0SG, U.K.
Tel: +44 (0)1938 810 128
www.colinette.com

Designer Yarns
Unit 8-10 Newbridge Industrial Estate, Pitt Street,
Keighley, West Yorkshire BD21 4PQ, U.K.
Tel: +44 (0)1535 664 222
www.designeryarns.uk.com
Debbie Bliss, Louisa Harding, and Noro.

Frog Tree
T&C Imports, PO Box 1119, 14 Frog Tree Lane,
East Dennis, MA 02641, U.S.A.
Tel: 508 385 8862
www.frogtreeyarns.com

ggh
Mühlenstraße 74, 25421 Pinneberg, Germany
Tel: +49 (0)4101 208 484
www.ggh-garn.de

Habu Textiles
135 West 29th Street, Suite 804, New York,
NY 10001, U.S.A.
Tel: 212 239 3546
www.habutextiles.com

Jade Sapphire
148 Germonds Road, West Nyack,
NY 10994, U.S.A.
Tel: 866 857 3897
www.jadesapphire.com

KnitGlobal
AC Wood Speciality Fibres, CCL House,
Inmoor Road, off Cross Lane, Tong,
Bradford BD11 2PS, U.K.
www.knitglobal.com

Knit One Crochet Too
91 Tandberg Trail, Unit 6, Wyndham,
ME 04062, U.S.A.
Tel: 800 357 7646
www.knitonecrochettoo.com

Lana Grossa
Heritage Stitchcraft Ltd, Redbrook Lane,
Brereton, Rugeley, Staffs WS15 1QU
Tel: +44 (0)1889 575 256
www.lanagrossa.com

Lantern Moon
7911 N.E. 33rd Drive, Suite 140, Portland,
OR 97211, U.S.A.
Tel: 800 530 4170
www.lanternmoon.com
Leigh Radford's Silk Gelato yarn.

Manos Del Uruguay
Sarl Distrilaine, 5 rue Thomas Edison,
44470 Carquefou, France
Tel: +33 (0)8 73 65 44 06
www.distrilaine.com

Ozark Handspun
PO Box 1405, Jefferson City,
MO 65102-1405, U.S.A.
Tel: 573 644 8736
www.ozarkhandspun.com

PluckyFluff
Web: www.pluckyfluff.com
Unique handspun yarns.

Rowan
Green Lane Mill, Holmfirth HD9 2DX, U.K.
Tel: +44 (0)1484 681 881
www.knitrowan.com
Rowan, Jaeger, and Gedifra yarns.

PILLOWS AND CUSHIONS
Allshapes Cushions Ltd
Unit 29, Vernon Building, Westbourne Street,
High Wycombe, Bucks HP11 2PX, U.K.
Tel: +44 (0)1494 465 581
www.allshapes.co.uk
*This company will make pillow forms to any size
and are very reliable; they have a helpful web site.*

LAVENDER
Norris & Armitage
3 Brooklands Road, Bedhampton, Havant,
Hants PO9 3NS, U.K.
Tel: +44 (0)2392 718 914
www.lavendersupplies.co.uk

*Two varieties of totally natural chemical-free
dried lavender from Provence, sold in resealable
bags from 9oz (250g) to 22lb (10kg).*

BEADS
*Check the Internet, as there are a lot of online
shops that sell all kinds of beads.*

Creative Beadcraft
20 Beak Street, London W1F 9RE, U.K.
Tel: +44 (0)20 7629 9964
www.creativebeadcraft.co.uk
Beads, sequins and trims.

BUTTONS
*Besides being functional, buttons can be used
as embellishments. You can use one stunning
huge one with other smaller elements (such as
small buttons, tiny pompoms, or beads), or use
beautiful vintage buttons in clusters or scattered
along an edge. For unusual or vintage examples,
try vintage-textile fairs, which are usually
advertised in local papers or craft and textile
magazines. You can also mooch around flea
markets, rummage sales, and secondhand shops.
Sometimes it's worth looking at secondhand
clothing just to see if the buttons are interesting—
you can cut them off and use them for your new
piece. Ebay is also a very good source for vintage
buttons and trims.*

The Button Queen
19 Marylebone Lane, London W1V 2NF, U.K.
Tel: +44 (0)20 7935 1505
www.thebuttonqueen.co.uk

Tender Buttons
143 E 62nd Street, New York, NY 10021, U.S.A.
Tel: 212 758 7004
*They don't have an online store, but it is, quite
simply, the best button shop I have ever been to
in the world. If you are ever anywhere near N.Y.C.,
make a beeline for it.*

RIBBONS AND TRIMS
Temptation Alley
359/361 Portobello Road, London W10 5SA, U.K.
Tel: +44 (0)20 8964 2004
www.temptationalley.com
*Very helpful and friendly store offering an
amazing selection of very reasonably priced
ribbons, trims, tassels, beads, feathers, sequins,
and lace. They ship worldwide.*

V V Rouleaux
102 Marylebone Lane, London W1U 2QD, U.K.
Tel: +44 (0)20 7224 5179
www.vvrouleaux.com
*Fantastic selection of ribbons and trims. There
are also V V Rouleaux stores in Sloane Square,
London; Glasgow; and Newcastle; and you can
buy online.*

**PURSE CLASPS AND BAG HANDLES
AND FRAMES**
Lacis
3163 Adeline Street, Berkeley, CA 94703, U.S.A.
Tel: 510 843 7178
www.lacis.com
*Fabulous selection of the most exquisite bag and
purse frames and handles. They have vintage
Lucite and other beauties.*

U-Handbag
150 McLeod Road, London SE2 0BS, U.K.
Tel: +44 (0)208 310 3612
www.u-handbag.com
*A useful website selling handbag and coin purse
frames, as well as bamboo, wood, metal, and
plastic bag handles of all shapes and sizes.*

Designers' Biographies

Julie Arkell is one of Britain's foremost contemporary folk artists. An avid collector, she recycles "the rejected debris of everyday life," using paper from old books, fabrics from vintage clothes, and objects that have been sourced from her local hardware and notions stores. Julie employs traditional techniques, such as papier-mâché, stitching, knitting, painting, embroidery, and collage, and through these evolving processes her exquisite "creatures" are made.

Debbie Bliss studied fashion and textiles at art college before becoming a knitwear designer. She has published more than 25 books of hand-knit designs for adults and children, and in 1999 she launched her own range of yarns.

When designing, Debbie loves to play with texture, combining, for example, the diagonals of a cable with the simplicity of a seed-stitch panel and using decorative stitch details to enhance a basic design. When she launched her own yarn range, it was natural to lean toward the traditional smooth yarns, which clarify texture and stitch, and to use beautiful fibers such as cashmere, alpaca, silk, and fine merino.
www.debbieblissonline.com

Ruth Cross was founded in 2004 by Ruth Bridgeman after she graduated with a degree in Fashion Textile Design from the University of Brighton, in England. Her focus now is to rethink the traditional capabilities of handknitting to create beautiful contemporary pieces. Ruth's creations are highly desirable; the stitches and techniques used are often unique to Ruth Cross, which makes their patterns highly distinctive and unusual. These pieces are impossible to copy using machines—for Ruth, it is all about the individual and their creative part in the process.
www.ruthcross.com

Nadine Curtis founded Be Sweet in 2003 while living in Cape Town, South Africa. Her previous experience in design and passion for socially conscious programs served as catalysts for turning her fascination with handmade accessories into a thriving business, which supports local women artisans in South Africa.

Be Sweet makes six different styles of luxury mohair in various blends, including brushed, bouclé, and baby mohair yarn. All yarn is hand-dyed and handspun, and many are offered in more than 60 solid colors and 15 handpainted colors. Select balls are accented with delicate ribbons, metallic strands, and African beads.

Bardet Wardell graduated from Rhode Island School of Design Apparel and held design positions in New York City with dress and sportswear manufacturers before producing her own labels, Bardet and Everyday Goddesses. With the advent of Be Sweet, Bardet has focused on creating patterns that are both beautiful and simple to execute with the unique yarns produced in South Africa.
www.besweetproducts.com

Kristeen Griffin-Grimes is a designer based in Washington State and creator of French Girl's hallmark style of knit and crochet patterns: ethereal, draped garments superbly fitting to the feminine form. French Girl patterns are constructed in a unique manner, the garments fashioned in one piece from start to finish. Using her seamstress and costuming background, Kristeen begins her design process almost architecturally, to deconstruct her envisioned garment and reconstruct it again in a more organic way, either from the top down, from the hem up, or from the back out.

The designer's aesthetic is rooted in her early years as a "nature girl" on her family's oyster farm on the rural Pacific Northwest coast.
www.frenchgirlknits.com

Louisa Harding studied Textiles for Fashion at Brighton University, in England. During her third year she undertook a placement at Rowan Yarns, who published two of her very early designs. After working in Canada she returned to England, where she worked as in-house designer for Rowan Yarns, selecting yarns, writing patterns, and contributing to its publications.

Since having children, she has been working alongside her husband Stephen, a photographer. Together they created the Miss Bea series of knitting books. As a result of the Miss Bea series, Louisa was given the opportunity of introducing her own line of yarns and pattern publications in 2005. She thoroughly enjoys the creative experience of playing with color, texture, and designing beautiful knitwear patterns.
www.louisaharding.co.uk

Claire Montgomerie has an M.A. in Constructed Textiles from the Royal College of Art, London. She has a wealth of experience in the craft and textile industries and runs a successful online business selling her quirky knitted wares. Claire teaches knitting classes at Loop, children's textile courses at the artsdepot, London, and textile jewelry courses at West Dean College, Sussex.

Claire is the author of *Easy Baby Knits* and the co-author of *London Crochet*. She has also contributed designs to *Hookorama*, *Instant Expert Crochet*, and *Loop: Vintage Crochet*.
www.clairemontgomerie.com

Leigh Radford is an award-winning author, designer and teacher living in the Pacific Northwest. Her books include the highly popular *AlterKnits: Imaginative Projects and Creativity Exercises* and *One Skein: 30 Quick Projects to Knit & Crochet*.

In 2006 Leigh created Silk Gelato, offering knitters a fiber with enhanced texture and plays of color for her unique pattern designs. Her enterprising efforts have resulted in a highly successful business collaboration with Lantern Moon, producers of Silk Gelato.

Leigh is in demand for her innovative classes and workshops. She enjoys teaching others the value of being creative and is inspired by the expression of original ideas that lend a fresh perspective to knitting and crochet.
www.leighradford.com

Kate Samphier was inspired by traditional knitting in Scotland, and her collections embrace Scottish knitwear manufacture, challenging tradition with an eclectic use of color, texture, and pattern.

After studying textiles in the Scottish Borders, Kate worked for a local woolen spinner for five years as a yarn and knit-fabric designer. Drawn to the raw material and colors that she worked with, Kate began to create her own knitted accessories to illustrate the versatility of the company's yarn ranges.

In Spring 2000 Kate set up her design studio and workshop. The following year, her first collection of knitted accessories was launched. Featured in magazines such as *Easy Living*, *Homes and Gardens*, *Junior*, and *Selvedge*, Kate's designs are for women with an eye for beauty and a quirky sense of style.
www.katesamphier.co.uk

Leslie Scanlon lives in a small New England coastal town with her husband and two children. She has been designing knitwear for ten years under the MAC & ME label. Her pieces are designed with clear colors and minimalist shapes in mind. Leslie combines elegant details with contemporary design to make timeless pieces.
www.macandme.net

Emma Seddon was taught to knit by her grandma, and has never looked back. She trained at Central St. Martins School of Art, London, where she did a Knitted Textiles degree. Working for the next 12 years on a variety of different textiles products, she spent most of her free time knitting, crocheting, and sewing, taking the odd spare moment to peruse thrift shops for patterns and balls of yarn.

In 2004 she became freelance, to pursue her first loves of knitting and crochet, and to inspire others to do the same, through teaching. She works with Rowan as a freelance design consultant, teaches at local schools for higher education, and works on a various design projects.

Nicky Thomson was inspired to knit as a young girl by her grandmother, Nellie Callear, having been enthralled by the clickety-clicks of her knitting needles and seeing the fabric magically appear. She loved rummaging in her grandmother's box of threads, buttons, and yarns, and learned to knit her first jumper. Totally hooked on textiles and yarns, she later studied for a B.A. in Textiles Design, specializing in woven and knitted fabrics. On graduating, she worked as an interior designer, but spent her free time designing and knitting.

In creating her designs, she constantly investigated color, pattern, the surface qualities of threads, and finishing techniques. She now works with a small U.K. manufacturing company to produce ever-changing collections, which are individually made and finished, and are sold worldwide.
www.nickythomson.com

Catherine Tough established her interior accessory design company in 2000 after graduating from the Royal College of Art, London. She sells her work throughout the U.K. and internationally. Much of the appeal of Catherine's knitwear comes from her reworking of traditional items and knitting patterns in luxury yarns, and revitalizing them with her contemporary stylings.

Catherine lives in Hackney, London, where she draws inspiration from the vibrant mix of urban cultures. Since her daughter Abigail was born, she has rediscovered much of her sense of color and playfulness, which first came from children's books, illustration, and imagination, and from her own rural Worcestershire childhood. This gives an intimate and friendly feel to her products, which appeal to adults and children alike. She has published two books, *Hip Knits* and *Easy Knits for Little Kids*.
www.catherinetough.co.uk

Nicki Trench founded Laughing Hens, a U.K. mail-order knitting web site, which has captured a new wave of interest in knitting as a modern creative hobby for women. Nicki has written two books, *The Cool Girl's Guide to Knitting* and *The Cool Girl's Guide to Crochet*, and is currently writing a third, *The Cool Girl's Guide to Sewing*.

Nicki's inspiration has always been color and texture, and she loves vintage designs in fabric and textile. The flowers, dots, and stripes represented in her designs draw from 1950s retro and 1960s color. Her background in wedding-cake design is reflected in her handknitting and crochet—opulent big roses and pretty, delicate flowers and leaves in yummy colored yarns that look good enough to eat.
www.laughinghens.com

Amy Twigger Holroyd is the designer of luxury knitwear label Keep & Share, for which she creates unconventional yet wearable pieces, each knitted on a chunky domestic machine in her Herefordshire workshop. Having first studied fashion design, she specialized in knitting, inspired by the potential for seamless three-dimensional shaping and the ability to create fabric and garment in one. Amy was taught to handknit by her grandmother as a child and created many weird and wonderful (usually half-finished) projects. The pattern in this book is her first foray for several years back into the world of handknitting and features a handknit version of her signature joining technique.
www.keepandshare.com

Juju Vail came to the U.K. in 1990 to study for an M.A. in Textile Design at St. Martins, after studying fashion and knitwear design in Montreal.

Since graduating, she has taught and written books and articles on many creative practices. These include quilting, sewing, beading, knitting, crochet, painting, and rug making.

Juju has a whim of iron and chronicles her creative passions on her blog. Her latest book is *Creative Beadwork*.
www.jujulovespolkadots.typepad.com

Donna Wilson graduated from the Royal College of Art, London, in July 2003. During her time there, she produced a range of work that included the "knitted friendly creatures," the "doily rug," "wrapped cacti," the "caterpillow" and the "hands on rug." The tactile quality of her work comes from her childhood in rural Scotland, where she developed a love for the organic form.

Donna's work is playful, tactile, and bright, inspired by the everyday oddities and deformities of life. She likes to think of each of her creations as a character in her very own wonderland, where scale and perception are toyed with.
www.donnawilson.com

Acknowledgments

This book would not be possible without the incredible work and involvement of so many people. I wish to express my thanks to all the talented designers who have contributed their creativity and sensibility to this project. The fact that you took time out of your already very hectic lives has truly touched me. From your yarns to your patterns, you are all shaping the world of knitting in a tremendous way.

A big "thank you" to my editor, Zia Mattocks, who, with her cool head, calmed me down in some of my more panicky moments and kept things ticking over. Thanks also to Barbara Zuñiga, a great book designer with a brilliant eye; I was fortunate indeed to have her contribute to this project. Thanks to Vanessa Davies, whose beautiful photography has brought the patterns to life. And to Pauline Hornsby, our brilliant pattern checker and technical editor. And of course, Jacqui Small, who thought of the book in the first place—thank you for approaching Loop and believing in the book and making it happen.

Thanks to Blue Sky Alpacas, Designer Yarns, ggh, Rowan, Jade Sapphire, Habu Textiles, and Be Sweet for their generosity and support (and for making such great yarns for knitters). Special thanks to Gina Wilde at Alchemy Yarns for making the time to dye her gorgeous yarns in the colors we needed.

My heartfelt thanks to the incredible staff at Loop. I have been blessed, right from the beginning, with warm, responsible, helpful women who happen to be great knitters as well. Thank you to Claire Montgomerie and Linda Marveng. Your grace and enthusiasm have made both the shop and this book a joy to do. Thanks also to Natalie Abbott and our talented teachers at Loop, whose patience, together with their passion for knitting, inspires us all: Aneeta Patel, Laura Long, Juju Vail, Julie Arkell, Bee Clinch, Jane Lithgow, and Emma Seddon. Thanks to Emerald Mosley, my brilliant website designer. And also, of course, thank you to all Loop's customers - we wouldn't be here without you.

To my dad, Jack Silverberg, and Joy, who like to mooch around the yarn fairs with me and have always been hugely supportive in numerous ways. And my mom, Joan Podel, Loop's biggest fan, whose enthusiasm has never waned.

I couldn't have done any of this book without the huge support behind the scenes from my dear husband, Steven, and our three children, Sonia, Niall, and Jonah. Over the course of a year they have been generous beyond belief and endlessly patient with a sometimes distracted partner and mom.

ADDITIONAL CREDITS

Photograph on page 7 copyright © Simon Brown, reproduced by kind permission.
www.simonbrownphotography.com

The publisher and author would also like to thank the following companies for kindly lending props for the photoshoot:

Grainne Morton
Tel: +44 (0)131 443 2755
www.grainnemorton.co.uk
Beautiful jewelry made with charms in silver casing

Seven & Eight Home
www.sevenandeighthome.co.uk

Sukie
Tel: +44 (0)1273 542 600
www.sukie.co.uk
Lovely quirky notebooks and other paper products

Vintage Heaven
Tel: +44 (0)1277 215 968
www.vintageheaven.co.uk

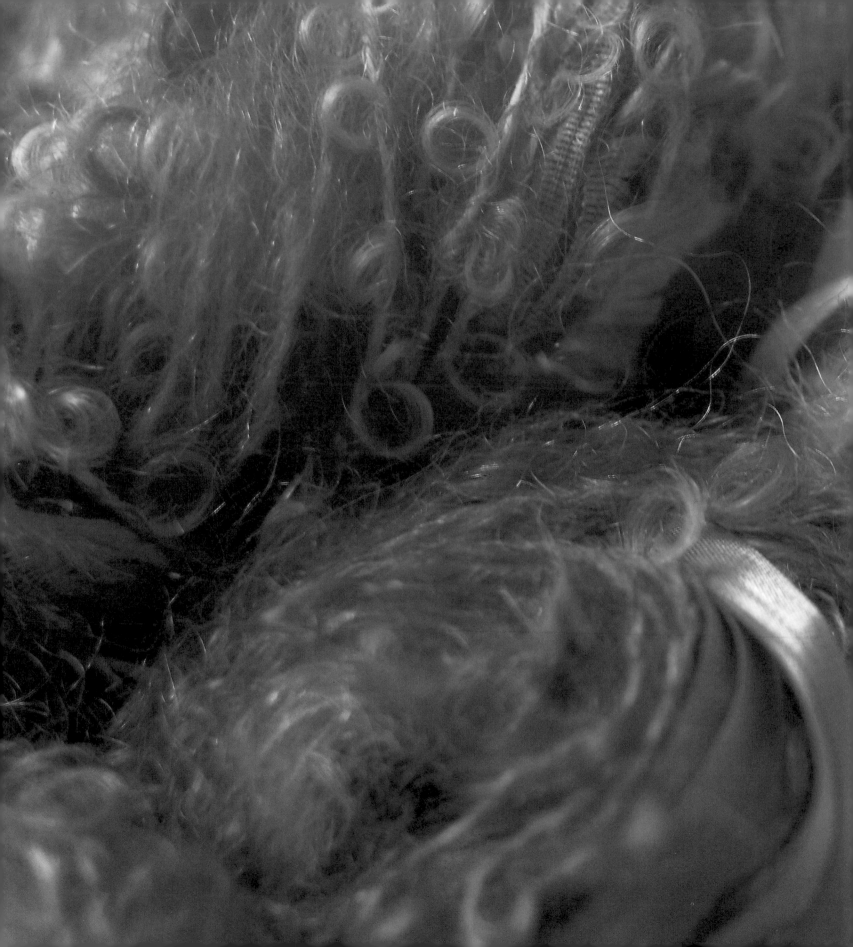